DISTINCTIVE WEDDINGS

About the author
Bláithín O'Reilly Murphy has enjoyed a long and varied career in events organisation and management. Following school she moved to London and worked as an air hostess, but always with an interest in and love of design, she returned to Dublin to study interior design and interior architecture in Limperts Academy through Portobello School, for which she received merits and distinctions. She worked for a number of years in domestic interior design, before moving into property management. Having been involved in arranging social and corporate events for the various companies she worked for, she decided to pursue a career in events management. She also completed a course in Wedding Planning and Event Management with the Fitzwilliam Institute. Together with her business partners James Murphy and Oisin O'Reilly, Bláithín founded Distinctive Weddings. She now works as a much sought-after wedding consultant alongside her team and lives in Lusk, Co. Dublin with her husband James.

Distinctive
Weddings

Tying the Knot without the Rope Burns!

Bláithín O'Reilly Murphy

VERITAS

Published 2008 by
Veritas Publications
7/8 Lower Abbey Street
Dublin 1
Ireland

Email publications@veritas.ie
Website www.veritas.ie

ISBN 978-1-84730-119-2

10 9 8 7 6 5 4 3 2 1

Information in chapter 4 by kind permission of David Greely.

A catalogue record for this book is available from the British Library.

Designed by Lir Mac Cárthaigh
Printed in Ireland by Betaprint Ltd, Dublin

Veritas books are printed on paper made from the wood pulp of managed forests. For every tree felled, at least one tree is planted, thereby renewing natural resources.

— Contents —

Acknowledgements

James — thanks for letting me go first! I love you so much.
Oisin — thanks for giving me the push to do this.
Mum — thanks for all your creative expertise.
Dad — thanks for steering me in the right direction.

Introduction

Congratulations!

WELL, YOU'RE GETTING MARRIED. Finally taking the plunge! The lure of His 'n' Hers bathrobes too powerful! At the moment the excitement of the engagement lingers, but soon preparations for the wedding day will have to be considered, and so will begin months of planning and organisation for your smooth and trouble-free day.

To say your wedding day is one of the most awe-inspiring and nerve-wracking of days is somewhat of an understatement. Having married recently, I can say that it wasn't until we were sat at the head table looking down on all our guests that my husband and I realised what it truly meant. Having pledged our lives to each other, this important event was shared with us by our family and friends, and we realised how blessed we were. Each and every person had chosen to travel, some thousands of miles, to be with us on this day. Seeing their happy faces made the effort, toil and expense that went into planning our big day all the more worthwhile.

Weddings are amazing, but they take time, research, effort and money! With most only marrying the once, few know how, where or even when to plan a wedding effectively or correctly. It can be a daunting experience, and as the day holds such high expectations, brides and grooms often put themselves under huge pressure to achieve the perfect day for themsevles and their guests.

I started writing this book because, while there are many excellent books on the market on wedding day preparations and getting married, when I was getting married I just wanted one that combined all the most helpful and relevant elements. Not wanting to do myself out of a job (I'm a wedding planner!), this book is designed to help you record, organise and experiment with your ideas all in one place. It is divided into five sections, and each chapter deals with a distinct part of either the marriage ceremony or wedding celebration. These chapters can also be read separately, or you can sit down and devour the entire book from start to finish! Either way, they are designed to deal with the aspect in question and any satellite issues that may spin off from them. These chapters also contain current facts and figures, and my own not inconsiderable experience and advice, as well as specialist advice garnered from my experience as a wedding planner. You will also see the occasional 'Remember ...' and 'Top Tip!' box. Appendices at the back of the book detail useful spreadsheets and information sheets, which will help you know what questions to ask when you come to organising any aspect of the day. Also included at the back are websites and contact details for appropriate vendors or suppliers that you may find useful, as well as examples of appropriate readings and gospels, possible music to be used during the ceremony, and a sample Mass booklet to point you in the right direction. The realistic, concise information found in this book will ease the pressure and provide you with practical advice for planning what will be the most magical day of your life.

While this book will aid you both on your journey to planning your big day, if you would like a professional hand please contact us today for your one-hour complimentary consultation (terms and conditions apply). *www.distinctiveweddings.ie.*

—Section One—
The Meaning of Marriage

— 1 —

Marriage, the Sacrament

What does it mean to you?

WHEN WE WERE YOUNG, we played 'mammies and daddies'. Most of us were obsessed with Barbie and Ken. Our teenage years were spent fantasising about the latest popular boy band, or the latest popular boy down the road. The college years were spent falling in love, and often quickly out of love again. And so it continues, until we meet the one we consider our perfect partner. All the while, we dream of that one day when it would all come together. Our wedding day, the dress, the car, the flowers, the reception … we imagine it all.

I often tell brides not to focus on the details but to remember what the day is all about. Few of us actually really sit and think about what it is we are doing in getting married. It's so easy to get caught up in choosing centrepieces, choirs and wedding cars, and while we put thought and effort into the flowers for the church and making sure each door is framed by a blooming rose tree, we seem to rarely really consider the importance of the ceremony itself. The exchanging of vows and the promises you will make before God and witnesses are far superior to your designer dress or S Class Merc or whether Auntie Mary bought you the entire Royal Doulton dinner set.

Marriage is defined as 'the social institution under which a man and woman establish their decision to live as husband and wife by legal commitments and/or religious ceremonies'. The Roman Catholic Church defines marriage thusly: 'Marriage is based on the consent of the contracting parties, that is, on their will to give themselves, each to the other, mutually and definitively, in order to live a covenant of faithful and fruitful love.'

A church wedding, distinct from a civil wedding, may not be for all. Johnny Doherty CSSR wrote:

> Every Church wedding automatically implies an awareness of God and a willingness to make God part of the relationship. This highlights one of the important elements of our faith as Catholics, namely that a marriage is a three-partner relationship that cannot work fully with only two. The presence of God in a couple's life together is vital so that they remain turned towards one another in love and so that their commitment to each other will grow ever stronger. ('Getting Married in the Catholic Church', www.gettingmarried.ie)

This can be difficult for couples who do not see themselves as religious, but it is an important element that every couple needs to take account of and develop in their lives.

The Church views the sacrament of marriage and the institution that it has become as a sacred and everlasting bond between two people, a man and a woman. The matrimonial union of man and woman is indissoluble; God himself has determined it: 'What therefore God has joined together, let no man put asunder.' Therefore, if 'till death do you part' is not what you had in mind for your marriage, a church wedding is not for you.

The *Catechism of the Catholic Church* explains marriage in the order of creation as follows:

The intimate community of life and love which constitutes the married state has been established by the Creator and endowed by him with its own proper laws ... God himself is the author of marriage. The vocation to marriage is written in the very nature of man and woman as they came from the hand of the Creator. Marriage is not a purely human institution despite the many variations it may have undergone through the centuries in different cultures, social structures and spiritual attitudes. These differences should not cause us to forget its common and permanent characteristics. Although the dignity of this institution is not transparent everywhere with the same clarity, some sense of the greatness of the matrimonial union exists in all cultures. The well-being of the individual person and of both human and Christian society is closely bound up with the healthy state of conjugal and family life.

God who created man out of love also calls him to love the fundamental and innate vocation of every human being. For man is created in the image and likeness of God who is himself love. Since God created him man and woman, their mutual love becomes an image of the absolute and unfailing love with which God loves man.

This can all seem very difficult to digest. Some people might have huge issues with allowing God and religion into something so (dare I use the word) sacred as their relationship and marriage.

Getting your head around it all may be difficult, so this might help. Imagine sitting in a park, on a hot summer's day, people lounging about enjoying the good weather, ice-creams in hand. Each person pretty similar to the next beside them; their lives could be yours and yours theirs; nothing seemingly different or extraordinary. Except one thing! You are sitting there alone, it would seem to all, but you know you are not alone – you've been chosen! Out of everyone there is in the world, the person you love has asked you to spend the rest of your life with them, through bad times and good. You are wrapped in the warm glow and loving feeling that for evermore your two lives will be joined as one and you will enter into the next stage of your life in unity. Now you are sat there alone, but yet you feel your bride- or groom-to-be beside you. The love that is between you surrounds you. You feel safe and secure, you feel loved and cherished – you feel God.

Now you may be thinking, hold on a second … I'm not religious – how did God wrangle his way into my life and now my marriage when I don't even pray, go to church or practice a religion? I suppose it all boils down to something over which you or I have no control, something that is far greater and which has existed far longer than we have, and that's the love our Heavenly Father has for us. Holy Scripture affirms that man and woman were created for one another: 'It is not good that the man should be alone.' The woman, 'flesh of his flesh', i.e. his counterpart, his equal, his nearest in all things, is given to him by God as a 'helpmate'; she thus represents God from whom comes our help. 'Therefore a man leaves his father and his mother and cleaves to his wife, and they become one flesh.' The Lord himself shows that this signifies an unbreakable union of their two lives by recalling what the plan of the Creator had been 'in the beginning': 'So they are no longer two, but one flesh.'

Church or civil?
Deciding now whether to have a church wedding or just a civil wedding is an important choice that must be made together. A civil wedding will make your marriage contract legally binding and is seen as a governmental institution. The 'civil marriage' does also take place during the church ceremony and Ireland is the only place in which both happen during the same ceremony. But like most contracts, civil marriages can be declared null and void with a divorce. A church wedding is seen as infinite and totally binding in the eyes of God, only ending when one spouse dies. And herein lies the uniqueness and 'romance' of a church wedding.

Fundamental to the wedding ceremony and marriage is Love. Love is what brings us, keeps us and holds us together. As previously established, God is love, and through his likeness so are we. As love is so integral to the ceremony and the marriage, we can see now how Johnny Doherty's statement – 'A Church wedding automatically implies an awareness of God and a willingness to make God part of the relationship' – is true.

A church wedding ceremony is the commitment made by the bride and groom to love one another 'for better or worse, in sickness and in health, all the days of our lives, until death do us part'. This small part of the ceremony really says it all ... can you honestly agree to do all that, with this one person? The commitment a couple makes to each other is so much more than words can express. That is why the sacrament of marriage is replete with symbolism.

Symbolism in the wedding ceremony
To explain the importance of symbolism within the ceremony, I will borrow an extract from *A Wedding of Your Own*, by Pádraig McCarthy. He writes:

> There is a saying attributed to the Chinese teacher, Lao-tzu: 'Those who know do not say; those who say do not know.' Fr Tony de Mello tells of students discussing this. When their teacher came in, they asked him what it meant. He said: 'Which of you knows the fragrance of a rose?' All the students indicated that they knew. The teacher said: 'Put it into words'. All of them were silent.

So much of marriage and Christian marriage is beyond words. Walking down the aisle, the tears of a mother, the lighting of a candle, an everlasting promise sealed with a kiss. The joy, the celebration, the feelings and emotions ... this is what we long for ... this is what we want. The dress, the cars and all the expense seem insignificant in that moment. The spirituality of the experience, the sense of community and the beginning of a new life together is what it is all about. Therefore, it is important to remember the enormity of the occasion for its spiritual and sacramental importance in our lives and not for any materialistic and monetary reasons.

Saying 'I Do'

Putting your feelings into words

AFTER THE DECISION has been made on whether to have a religious or civil ceremony (more on this in a minute), attention is then brought to the ceremony content and saying 'I do'. These two innocent little words, when combined, form an unbreakable bond that unites two lives together forever. They are two of the most frightening, yet unassuming words that can ever be uttered together.

Whether and when you have decided on a religious or civil ceremony, there are still yet more decisions to be made. Prayers, readings, music and participants all still need to be decided upon.

Civil ceremony
The civil ceremony is possibly the easier of the two to organise. They are generally considerably shorter, ranging from ten to twenty-five minutes in length, and can, if you wish, come 'no frills attached'. Generally with a civil ceremony, the 'prayers', readings and music choices are non-religious in their content and meaning, and act only to personalise your ceremony. As many civil ceremonies are conducted by one registrar in a given

day, often one after the other, it is important to check on your 'allotted' time before putting huge effort into creating what might become a lengthy civil ceremony. Do bear in mind that the tradition of being slightly late to the wedding may not be possible with a civil ceremony. Often ceremonies run concurrently, and if you miss your allocated time you may have to reschedule for another day. See Chapter 3, 'Marriage and the Law', or Chapter 7, 'Location, Location, Location', for supplementary information on registry office ceremonies.

Before getting down to the nitty-gritty of a religious ceremony, let us first talk about marriage preparation courses and pre-nuptial enquiries.

Marriage preparation courses

If a church wedding is something that both you and your fiancé are working towards, a marriage preparation course is most likely one of the items on your 'to do' list, up there with registering the marriage. It is the responsibility of the priest to ensure that both bride and groom are ready and prepared for the sacrament of marriage. It is a monumental step in life, one with an unbreakable bond in the eyes of the church. One way of ensuring that a couple are ready and truly understand the enormity of marriage and what to expect is for them to attend one of these courses. They run nationwide and are generally carried out over a weekend or over the course of a few evenings. Some priests insist that such a course be completed before they will marry a couple. Others are prepared to consider alternative options. It is important to check with your specific priest on his preference. Marriage preparation courses are available from a number of agencies: the most reputable and widely know is ACCORD (www.accord.ie) which provides services on all aspects of marriage and family life, including marriage preparation, counselling and family planning.

Pre-nuptial enquiries

In addition to making sure that both bride and groom are prepared for marriage, a priest must also satisfy himself that both parties are free to marry. This is normally established during the pre-nuptial enquiry. A pre-nuptial enquiry is a formal meeting between the couple and their current parish priest (who may not necessarily be the priest that will marry them). The enquiry establishes that you are both willing Catholics who are free to marry and intend to live and bring up any children you may have as Catholics (and because Catholicism is the predominant religion here in Ireland, all information on the marriage ceremony will relate back to it. For information on requirements pertaining to the marriage ceremony of other religions, please see Chapter 3, pp. 32–33). During the 'enquiry' you will be asked a number of questions on your faith, your family, your beliefs, and you will be asked to produce these four documents:

* *Certificate of Baptism*
* *Certificate of Confirmation*
* *Letter of Freedom*
* *Death Certificate (should you be re-marrying after the death of a spouse).*

The first two *certificates* will be available from the churches in which you were baptised and confirmed. A phone call or letter to the relevant parish office giving your full name, parents' names and possibly sponsors, along with the relevant dates of both events, is generally sufficient to have them sent out. A *letter of freedom* is required from every parish in which you have resided for longer than six months since you were eighteen and states that you did not marry in that parish while resident there. The letter again comes from the priest or parish office of each parish you have resided in for six+ months. Often this can be a time-consuming and lengthy process, especially if you were not known to the priest or parish during your residency. Signing a sworn affidavit in the presence of a Justice of the Peace can often suffice in the instance that there are too many letters to obtain or they prove difficult in getting.

Remember ...

A pre-nuptial enquiry is not to be confused with a pre-nuptial agreement, which is a legal document signed by both parties in advance of the wedding and is normally concerned with division of money, children and assets in the event of a divorce.

The ceremony: choices and content

And now to the ceremony itself. It is strange to think that the wedding ceremony is possibly the most overlooked part of the day, yet, without it, the day wouldn't happen. I often have brides who, once they have the ceremony location and decoration sorted, rarely give the ceremony another thought. Some even delegate the reading or music choices to the priest or a member of their family. Do you think the same brides would be so cavalier with their wedding dress? I think not!

In an ideal world, as Catholics we would be attending Mass and ceremonies from the day we were born, with exceptions being made when we were 'in bed with the doctor', as my Granny used to say. It's not an ideal world, and most likely the majority of you stopped attending regular Mass when you were confirmed, and now 'pop in' for Christmas, Easter, christenings, weddings and funerals, much like myself. But however sporadic your attendance, this is still one of the most important ceremonies you will take part in during your life and it should be treated as such.

Often, because of their lack of experience with such a ceremony, brides and grooms don't know where to start. This may seem like the obvious thing to do, but speaking to your priest is the best place to begin. He will first be able to guide you on the appropriate type of ceremony for your wedding. Within the church these fall into two general types. The first, *a marriage within a Eucharistic celebration*, is suitable for those of the same Christian denomination or for those whose churches are in communion. The second, *a simple marriage ceremony*, is suited to those who do not wish to exclude guests from receiving communion.

My couples often find the thought of designing their wedding ceremony overwhelming and almost impossible. Part of this is possibly due to the fact that while they have faith and belief in God (hence the church wedding), they don't consider themselves religious and so the thoughts of creating a religious wedding ceremony is beyond them.

To make the creation of the ceremony easier to understand, let us consider the ceremony in its Mass booklet format. This is the booklet that is produced to guide you, your family and your priest through the wedding ceremony. You'll be pleased to know that your wedding ceremony will follow the existing ceremony outlines set by the church and yours will be made unique by your reading, prayer and music choices. Opposite are outlines for a marriage ceremony containing a Eurcharistic celebration, and a simple marriage ceremony. And at the back of the book, in Appendix iii, a sample of a Mass booklet is given for your guidance.

Think of each heading as a checklist for a prayer, reading or piece of a ceremony you have yet to decide on.

Marriage within a Eucharistic Celebration

INTRODUCTORY RITE
Greeting
Introduction
Penitential Rite
Opening Prayer

LITURGY OF THE WORD
Readings chosen from Scripture
Sermon

CELEBRATION OF MARRIAGE
The Address and Questions to the Couple
The Exchange of Rings
The Exchange of Consent
Prayers of Intercession

LITURGY OF THE EUCHARIST
Preparation of the Gifts
Eucharist Prayer
Communion Rite

CONCLUDING RITE
Solemn Blessing or Prayer
Sending Forth
Signing of the Register

Simple Marriage Ceremony

INTRODUCTORY RITE
Greeting
Introduction
Opening Prayer

LITURGY OF THE WORD
Readings chosen from Scripture
Sermon

CELEBRATION OF MARRIAGE
The Address and Questions to the Couple
The Exchange of Consent
The Exchange of Rings
Prayers of Intercession
The Lord's Prayer
Nuptial Blessing

CONCLUDING RITE
Solemn Blessing or Prayer
Sending Forth
Signing of the Register

The general outline of content is already predefined and your ceremony will be made unique by your specific choices. It is important to remember that while this is your ceremony and should be largely based on your choices as a couple, your priest will also be instrumental in helping you design your wedding ceremony. He will obviously be able to provide you with numerous books and bibles from which to choose readings and gospels. There are also numerous publications on the market specifically designed to help you choose appropriate fillings for the various options. Three such books are *Readings for Your Wedding* (Veritas, 1995) by Brian Magee, *A Wedding of Your Own* (Veritas, 2003, 4th edition) by Pádraig Mc Carthy and *On The Way To The Wedding* (Veritas, 2006) by Elizabeth Hughes. Appendix 1 on p. 163 gives an outline of some of the most popular readings and gospels chosen by couples for the marraige ceremony.

A really handy way of choosing your readings and devising your Mass booklet is given on *www.gettingmarried.ie*. This recently launched website is an invaluable tool when making your choices for your wedding ceremony. We used this site ourselves, both creating separate accounts and making our own choices. When we had each completed a booklet (over the period of a few weeks) we sat down to decide on which choices to go ahead with. We were actually surprised at the number of times we had both chosen the same reading or prayer, which was great as then there were few arguments over whose choice got picked!

Other factors

LANGUAGE

It might seem odd, but language choice is a consideration. Beyond our now ever-present multi-nationality status, Ireland is a bilingual state, if a little one-sided in its choice of language. While English may be more widely spoken, Irish is our mother tongue. Integrating prayers or songs in Irish into the ceremony is a lovely nod to your heritage. Another option is of course to have the wedding ceremony conducted in Latin. Most of us are probably too young to remember, but up until a few decades ago all church ceremonies and masses were conducted through Latin, and while many of your own friends may be sitting there thinking, 'I thought they were both Irish? Why are they having the ceremony in French/Spanish/Chinese?' it would definitely be a unique point as few choose this option. When making your choice, do consider those who will be involved and whether they have the skills to partake in such a ceremony.

My own husband is from the Gaeltacht area of Mayo, and growing up in a strong traditional Irish home and attending the local Gaelscoile myself, it felt only natural for us to incorporate Irish into our wedding ceremony. As we had a number of guests from England, Germany and Australia, we thought it best not to conduct the entire ceremony in Irish but instead had a selection of Prayers of the Faithful and hymns in Irish. It was a surprise for our foreign guests and welcomed by those who speak the mother tongue daily.

READINGS AND PARTICIPATION OF GUESTS

As you would expect, the wedding ceremony is largely focused on the bride and groom, and is performed by your priest. (It is probably important at this stage to point out that the priest does not marry the bride and groom: they perform this part of the ceremony themselves and it is they who marry each other.) In addition to these principle characters, other guests will be involved in the ceremony too.

When choosing readers for your ceremony, make sure they will be comfortable to perform a reading and that they will be articulate and clear. They don't need to be professional speakers, just able to read loudly and clearly enough for all to hear and understand. After all, there is no point in going to all the trouble of creating a lovely wedding ceremony if your friends and family mumble their way through the prayers and readings. Asking them well in advance and providing them with their reading as soon as possible will give them loads of time to prepare and practice. Make sure they attend the rehearsal ceremony – this will also give you an opportunity to hear them in advance and make suggestions (nice ones) if required. They will also be glad of the chance to see where and how their reading will take place.

As well as including family and friends in your ceremony by asking them to do a reading or a prayer, you can also involve them as ushers, ministers of the Eucharist, altar servers and musicians. You can of course explore other areas with your priest, such as giving the gifts and even ringing the church bells, if you want to involve a large number of people.

Remember ...
For specific jobs, such as ministers of the Eucharist or altar service, those family members or friends chosen must be practicing ministers or servers in their own parishes.

MUSIC OCCURRENCES

Your music selection should be appropriate for church and suitable for the part of the ceremony it is to accompany. Music is normally played/sung at the following points:

※ *Entrance Hymn*
※ *Responsorial Psalm*
※ *Gospel Acclamation*
※ *Preparation of Gifts (Offertory Procession)*
※ *Sign of Peace*
※ *Communion Hymn*
※ *Communion Reflection*
※ *Recessional Hymn*
※ *Signing of the Register*

Liturgically correct (church approved) hymns are your best choice. Your priest and chosen music professional will be able to advise you on the appropriate choices. Some music samples suitable for your ceremony are given in Appendix II, p. 167.

Remember …

A church is a solemn and dignified place. Your wedding sacrament is an important and sombre ceremony. Your choices (in all areas) should reflect this. Inappropriate humour, song, prayer or reading choices should be kept for the reception. It is important to work with your priest on your choices as there are certain elements (songs, readings, poems) you may consider appropriate but which may not be allowed.

Your wedding ceremony, whether religious or civil, should reflect you both as a couple and should pave the way for your new life together. Wedding ceremonies are a celebration of love, life and happiness and are all about the joining of two families and new beginnings. Family involvement and special meaning will make yours all the more intimate and memorable.

— SECTION TWO —
The Practicalities

— 3 —

Marriage
and the Law

Meeting the legal requirements

Iᴛ's ᴀʟᴡᴀʏs ᴛʜᴇ ʙɪɢɢᴇsᴛ ꜰᴇᴀʀ that you will go to all the trouble and expense of planning a wedding, only to discover days either before or after the event that it isn't/wasn't legal. Not that you hear of it happening often … but it is definitely not an area you want to leave to chance.

As with most legal requirements, until you find yourself in a situation of having/needing to know, you rarely have an idea of what is involved. Reliable, informed, up-to-date information is essential in this area.

The following information has been taken and adapted from the website *citizensinformation.ie* to give you as much detail on the various options and requirements open to both resident and non-resident couples wishing to marry in Ireland. They are correct at time of print, but as with all laws are subject to change, and so it is always advisable to double-check all details with your priest/registrar/wedding planner in advance.

Requirements for marriage

If you are an Irish citizen normally resident in Ireland, you must be at least eighteen years old to get married. There are some exceptions to this; please consult: *www.citizensinformation.ie*. Essentially, the age rule is the same, irrespective of whether you partake in a religious ceremony or civil ceremony. In addition, you must have the capacity to marry. That is, you must freely consent to marriage and have the capacity to understand what marriage means.

Notification requirements for marriage

Since 5 November 2007, anyone marrying in the Republic of Ireland (irrespective of whether they are an Irish citizen or a foreign national) must give three months' notification before they marry. You must make this notification in person to the registrar in the district where you intend to marry. On making contact with the registrar, they will inform you of what documentation you need to bring with you, but generally you will be required to present:

- *Passport or driving licence as identification*
- *PPS number*
- *Original final decrees in respect of all and any previous divorces*
- *Death Certificate if either party is widowed.*

You will also have to pay a notification fee of €150. Find out more on *www.citizensinformation.ie*.

In addition to their personal particulars the couple will need to provide the following details:

- *Intended date of marriage*
- *Whether it is to be a civil or religious ceremony*
- *The names and dates of birth of their witnesses*
- *The details of their proposed solemniser and venue.*

When the registrar is satisfied that all documentation is complete, intact and correct and that the couple are free to marry, a Marriage Registration Form (MRF) is issued. Without the MRF the marriage is not effectively legal. It is required whether you are having a civil or religious ceremony.

REGISTRY OFFICE WEDDINGS

Registry offices open from 9 a.m. to 5 p.m., Monday to Friday only, so it is not possible to have a registry office wedding at the weekend. They are also *very* strict on time – so, as mentioned before, if the bride observes the tradition of arriving late, you are likely to miss your time slot, which means the whole process must start again.

CHURCH WEDDINGS

If you wish to marry in a Roman Catholic or Church of Ireland (Anglican) church or some other church, the residency requirements above do not apply (but obviously the notification requirements do). The actual requirements vary between different religions.

The guidelines below are just a brief overview of the situation in each church. This is a complex area and you would do well to seek a consultation with the relevant religious leader or church head of the religion in which you wish to marry.

Roman Catholic

If both parties are Catholic and are marrying for the first time, or have been widowed, getting married in a Catholic church is relatively straightforward. You will need 'letters of freedom' from every parish in which you have previously lived or a legal affidavit declaring your freedom to marry. Paperwork is completed in your home parish, not in the parish where you will marry.

If either the bride or groom is not Roman Catholic but you wish for the marriage to take place in a Roman Catholic church, a dispensation must be obtained from the Bishop. This is usually granted on the basis that all future children will be baptised and brought up in the Catholic faith.

Church of Ireland
One party to the marriage *must* be Anglican or Episcopalian. If you meet this requirement you need to contact the vicar in the parish in which you plan to marry, who will then advise you on other requirements.

Inter-Church Marriage
If either the bride or groom is not Roman Catholic, but wish for the marriage to take place in a Roman Catholic church, a dispensation must be obtained from the Bishop.

Presbyterian/Methodist
Marriage in either of these churches is at the discretion of the local minister. Religious affiliation is not always required, though you will have to meet with and satisfy the minister of your sincerity and of your freedom to marry.

Jewish
Both parties to the marriage must be Jewish and permission to marry is at the discretion of the chief rabbi. You will be required to meet in person with the rabbi at the synagogue at which you wish to marry before permission is granted and to bring with you letters of introduction from your own rabbi.

Society of Friends (Quakers)
Both parties must be members of the Society of Friends, be free to marry and of age. You will be required to meet in person with the elders in the area in which you wish to marry.

Remember ...
If you are a member of any religion other than those listed above, you cannot legally marry in a church in Ireland. If you do marry in another faith you will need to have a civil (registry office) wedding also in order for the marriage to be registered by the state.

What if I have been married before?

If either of you have been married previously, you will have to produce a Divorce Decree Absolute or a Death Certificate, as appropriate, in order to marry in *either* a registry office or in those churches that permit remarriage of divorced persons. This information will be given to the registrar when you are notifying of your intention to marry.

In the case of Catholic weddings, marriage of divorced persons who previously married in the Catholic Church is not possible, even if the civil marriage has been dissolved. The Roman Catholic Church does not recognise divorce; you can only re-marry if a previous marriage was annulled by the Church and you have had a civil divorce.

The Jewish religion does recognise divorce, and permission to marry will be at the discretion of the chief rabbi. Quakers too recognise divorce.

Many couples who, because of their personal circumstances, are not allowed to marry in a church choose to have a civil marriage, either in Ireland or in their own country, and then have a church blessing in Ireland.

Can we marry on the beach/on a cliff/by a dolmen?

The short answer is no. But you can marry in any pre-approved building in Ireland; this means that you can get married in a castle should it fall under this remit – however, it is not possible at present to get married on a beach, on a cliff or by a dolmen. Go to Chapter 7 for supplementary information on marriage in a pre-approved building.

There are certain restrictions as to the location of the wedding such as those listed below:

> ※ *The ceremony room must have adequate capacity to accommodate, comfortably seated, the numbers attending the ceremony.*

✳ *There must be unrestricted public access without charge to the venue.*

✳ *The venue must have adequate public liability insurance.*

✳ *The place in which the marriage is to be solemnised must be a fixed structure that is clearly identifiable by description and location as a distinct part of the venue.*

Remember ...
This is intended as a *guide only* on the legal requirements for marrying in Ireland and is correct at the time of printing. However, it is suggested that you clarify that you have satisfied all requirements yourself by checking with your priest and the relevant authorities.

Registrar of marriages

You can contact the county registrar offices at the numbers below. If you are calling from outside Ireland, prefix each number with the country code for Ireland (oo 353) and then drop the first 'o' from the numbers given below.

County	Telephone No.	County	Telephone No.
Carlow	0509 913 1664	Limerick	061 483763
Cavan	049 433 1530	Longford	043 46410
Clare	064 682 1041	Louth	042 340 66
Cork	021 270508	Mayo	094 9021 522
	021 276558	Meath	046 9431 209
Donegal	074 918 711	Monaghan	047 823 88
Dublin	01 8725555	Offaly	0506 212 05
	Ext. 4806	Roscommon	090 6626 132
Galway	091 5623 40	Sligo	071 914 2228
Kerry	066 712 1998	Tipperary	052 21195
Kildare	045 897 348	Waterford	051 874 144
Kilkenny	056 775 1702	Westmeath	044 483 15
Laois	0502 21340	Wexford	053 223 29
Leitrim	061 414 655	Wicklow	0404 673 61

— 4 —

The Rock

The art behind buying the ring

NEVER ASSUME OR EXPECT ANYTHING when planning a wedding. With this in mind, we will neither assume nor expect that you are engaged or have an engagement ring. Many couples nowadays discuss and plan their wedding months in advance of their engagement and so you may very well be on your way to wedded bliss and have still to get the ring!

A short history lesson on engagement rings
The use of engagement rings dates back to 1215. They were initially simple bands, similar to our modern-day wedding band. With time, the use of jewels and precious gems were incorporated into the rings. At first, law forbade any middle or lower class people from using jewels or gems in their rings as they denoted status and power; however, over time this law relaxed and it became common place (where affordable) for anyone to use precious stones.

It is tradition in the western world that the engagement ring be worn on the forth finger of the left hand, commonly known as the ring finger. This stemmed from the belief during classical times that this finger contained the *vena amoris* or 'vein of love'. The use of diamonds in engagement rings is a more recent occurrence and came about during the Middle Ages. One of the first occurrences of the diamond engagement (or wedding) ring can be traced back to the marriage of Maximilian I (then Archduke of Austria) to Mary of Burgundy in 1477. The diamond engagement ring did not become the standard it is considered today until after an extensive marketing campaign by De Beers in the middle of the twentieth century, which came to include one of the most famous advertising slogans: 'A Diamond is Forever.'

In the early twentieth century, the United States jewellery industry attempted to start a trend of male engagement rings, going so far as to create a supposed 'historical precedent' dating back to medieval times. The attempt failed, although the industry applied lessons learned from this venture in its more successful bid to encourage the use of male wedding rings. With this said, it is the custom in some countries for both the bride and groom to wear engagement rings, although it is most likely that the groom's engagement ring will later become his wedding band.

How much to spend?
Deciding on the cost of an engagement ring is like trying to decide the length of a piece of string! It has been suggested that the cost of an engagement ring should be two months of the groom-to-be's salary ... again, this is yet another clever marketing ploy developed by De Beers during their marketing campaign. It does, however, give a rough idea as to what you can expect to spend.

The cost of the ring will be defined by what you are prepared to pay for it, and its worth defined by the four Cs: Cut, Colour, Clarity and Carat.

The four Cs explained

CUT refers to the shape, proportion and finish of the stone. A badly cut diamond will not refract light properly, making the stone look lifeless. Most common cuts include brilliant (round), princess (square), emerald (rectangular) and oval.

COLOUR refers to the lack of colour in the stone. It is graded from D at the top of the scale to Z at the bottom. D,E and F are referred to as exceptional white, G,H and I as white, J and K as slightly tinted, and below that as tinted. Colour can be affected by fluorescence, as can value. Fluorescence in a high colour can devalue, and in a low colour increase the value, and colour can only be determined using a special 'dialite' light.

CLARITY is the amount of inclusion in the stone, or internal marks. These can be black or clear, and are referred to as IF, VVS1-2, VS1-2, SL1-2, P1-2-3, depending on their size and position. A lot of inclusion will block light travelling through the stone, so the stone will be duller if it is bad. Clarity is always rated using a 10x triplet loupe (an extremely high quality, ochromatic magnifying lens used to magnify and identify rocks, minerals, insects, stamps, coins etc.).

CARAT is the actual weight of the stone. 1 carat = .2 grams. Prices will jump at the ½ and full carat marks, and sometimes at the ¼ carats. Also, small diamonds aren't 'chips'; often the same amount of cutting work has gone into them as bigger stones.

In addition, *certificates* are the 'passports' for a gemstone, stating all of the above. There are about forty companies who certify stones, and of these, only a handful's certificates are worth the paper they're printed on. A popular myth is that if a stone doesn't have a cert it isn't a diamond. This is rubbish. There are a lot of beautiful stones out there that aren't certified, and a lot of stones where the quality doesn't make the cost of certification viable. Generally, if the salesperson is trained, they can tell you what you need to know by looking at the diamond.

Conflict diamonds are those whose sale are used to fund wars, and are illegal to trade. The term applies to some diamonds from around 1990 onwards. Don't worry too much about this, as most traders will have letters from their suppliers stating that they are 'conflict free', who will in turn have letters from their suppliers, and so on up the chain.

The *metals* used in diamond-set rings are usually gold and platinum. American and Continental setting are often 14kt gold, whilst Ireland and Britain are more inclined toward 18kt. Pure gold is 24kt, which is never, despite popular belief, used to manufacture jewellery, as it is much too soft. Eighteen kt gold is a mixture of eighteen parts gold to six parts other metals to give it strength and colour. White gold is eighteen parts gold to six parts metals such as palladium, which gives it a whiter appearance. However, the predominant colour is still yellow, so the ring is rhodium plated. This plating may need to be redone every couple of years (depending on how good the plating has been done initially, and what kind of wear the ring is getting), and should cost no more than €50. Platinum is a completely different, harder metal, and also more expensive than gold. Eighteen kt gold rings are sometimes stamped '750', 14kt stamped '585' and platinum '950'.

If you are *buying abroad*, bear in mind that the difference in price is generally the taxes charged in the country you're buying in. Retailers in Ireland have to pay 21 per cent VAT and tax on their end-of-year profit. Not so in the likes of Dubai. Also bear in mind that a lot of the cut qualities of stones bought abroad aren't particularly good, and settings are also often not particularly well made. At least when you buy in Ireland you can go back to the shop you bought it in if you have a problem.

Now that you are armed with the technical information, consider the practical elements of buying an engagement ring.

Ring practicalities

Bear in mind that you will wear this ring for the remainder of your life, that its look, feel, height, shape, colour and size will be something that you see every day. Having gone through three engagement rings before finally making it up the aisle, I will give you my tuppence worth.

Before my husband and I became engaged we talked about how, where and when we would buy the ring. After all, it is a pretty big purchase, one I know I waited for most of my life! At the time, money was tight: we were both only out of college, had just put a deposit on our house and really didn't have a huge amount to spend.

Our first purchase was online, and we got amazing value for money, paying about €800 for a ring valued at €3,000+! However, I quickly realised that the materialistic side of me was more prominent than I had previously thought, and while I had gone for quality, I really wanted quantity! In essence, my lovely ring that I had said yes to ... was too small! I will not say that our seller misrepresented the ring – not in the slightest. He was very exact with the measurements, sizes and provided numerous pictures. I just thought that it would be bigger! I never actually took out the ruler and drew the measurements he provided.

But bless my hubby-to-be, he understood, and so, months into our engagement, he bought me ring number two (don't tell his mother!) This one was everything I wanted ... it was my original ring, only bigger! It had sparkle, it had shine and, more importantly, it had big diamonds! But sadly, getting what you want doesn't always turn out the way you want it. Within two months the band on the ring had snapped, so we returned it to be repaired. And within six months of that I had lost a whole carat! Driving along one day we noticed an entire diamond was gone, never to be found. The bridge on my ring had fallen or been knocked and one whole diamond had been lost forever. I was sick! Lucky for us, we were insured up to the hilt! But a second fault with the ring was too much for me. I considered it jinxed and insisted the jeweller take it back, and we went elsewhere.

And so we arrived at ring number three! I now knew I needed to be realistic ... and was counting on that old mantra – third time lucky! I finally chose an unusual antique setting, with a low mount with several different cuts. My ring is definitely not what you would call your typical engagement ring, but then again, neither was coming to the decision to buy it!

So with your mind now filled with historical facts, technical trivia and my life experience nonsense, go forth and purchase your ring!

Remember ...

Really think about what you want. Even buy some costume rings and wear them to see how they look, feel and work with your life. Shop around and do try alternatives, but you can't beat seeing and holding the ring before you buy. And insure, insure, insure — get your ring on the house insurance or its own policy ... it could save you both a lot of heartache.

Save the Date

When to get married?

DECIDING ON YOUR WEDDING DATE really solidifies proceedings. The date you choose will impact most other areas of your wedding and there are several things to consider:

- *The season*
- *The month*
- *The day of the week*
- *Sporting events*
- *Holidays*
- *Public holidays*
- *Family events.*

Some brides or grooms have always had a specific date or month in mind of when they would like to get married. For me, I always wanted to get married during the summer, my husband in July because it's his favourite month, and on the seventh because seven is his lucky number and hence we married on 7 July 2007 … now he has no excuse for forgetting our anniversary! Choosing a special date that means something to both of you is always a nice idea, or a combination of important numbers adds to the occasion and reduces the risk of forgotten anniversaries.

Year, season, month, day

The easiest thing to do first is decide on the year. With buying houses, saving for weddings and starting careers, brides and grooms are often planning their weddings two to five years in advance, maybe even longer! You may think that taking two years to plan a wedding is far too much time, but believe me, even with two years, we found it difficult to find available venues and suppliers. We visited thirteen different venues before we found one that was available on our wedding date, and that was eighteen months before our wedding!

It's never too early to plan. Some venues and suppliers will take bookings for up to five years away, although they may not be able to supply you with pricing until a year or two in advance of your date.

Once you have decided on the year, the next thing is the season and month. Weddings happen all year round and each month has its own charms.

Marry when the year is new, he'll be loving, kind and true.
When February birds do mate, you wed nor dread your fate.
If you wed when March winds blow, joy and sorrow both you'll
*   know.*
Marry in April if you can, joy for maiden and for man.
Marry in the month of May, you will romance the day.
Marry when June roses grow and over land and sea you'll go.
Those who in July do wed must labour for their daily bread.
Whoever wed in August be, many a change is sure to see.
Marry in September's shine so that your life is rich and fine.
If in October you do marry, love will come but riches tarry.
If you wed in bleak November, only joys will come, remember!
When December's snows fall fast, marry and your love will last.
— OLD LORE

Traditionally the summer months are the most popular. This has long since been the case, and perhaps dates back to the Middle Ages when people generally only bathed once a year. The annual bath took place in May or June and couples would marry in the days and weeks that followed so that they would smell nice and fresh and be presentable on their wedding day.

Another reason for the popularity of summer weddings are the longer, hotter, brighter days and abundance of bank holidays. It is also the traditional time for people to take holidays from work and so couples find it easier to take time themselves and their guests find it easier to travel if they live abroad. Because of this, the summer months are known as the High Season (this stretches from May to September). Prices are higher and venues and suppliers are harder to secure due to popularity. There are, of course, ways and means of getting around this. For example, marrying on a weekday is generally cheaper than a Friday or Saturday, with some venues offering special midweek deals (although these 'special rates' can generally be availed of midweek all year round).

Christmas is another popular time of year. This is due to the beauty and decoration of the festive season, and often the added bonus of many family and friends being around for a period of time.

Every season and month has its own uniqueness and offers special treats, decorations, flowers and suitability of venues, themes and colours. No matter when you choose, you will not be able to find a year, month, date and day that suits everyone. It is important that your key people are available; after that, everyone else that comes is a bonus! Making a list of upcoming events or times of year during which you do not want to get married will help narrow things down. Other areas to consider when selecting your date are location, budget, theme and colours. A beach wedding with pastel colours and Hawaiian-inspired decor in the depths of winter may not work as well as you had hoped! And your budget may not stretch to the most picturesque castle during the summer months, but you might be able to afford it on a Monday in April or October.

As with the time of year, the day of the week you choose will also have an impact.

> *Monday for wealth,*
> *Tuesday for health,*
> *Wednesday best day of all,*
> *Thursday for losses,*
> *Friday for crosses,*
> *and Saturday no luck at all.*
> — OLD LORE

Fridays, Saturdays and bank holiday weekends are generally the most popular and therefore the most expensive. These are also the easiest times for your guests to travel and take time off work, which can add to the difficulty in securing one day or the other, unless you are working well in advance. Putting your name down for a cancellation can be a risky business and makes it much more difficult to make definite arrangements or plans.

Remember ...
Be sure to think of and consider any upcoming sporting, political or religious events that may interfere with your selected date, as they may explain why the date at your exclusive venue isn't already booked!

Once you have set the date, you can start the countdown and get on with the planning! There's a handy chart given at the back in Appendix IV, p. 184 to aid in your date decision.

— 6 —

Money Matters

Can you afford to get married?

WEDDINGS ARE WHAT DREAMS ARE MADE OF. Most little girls sit and fantasise about flowing white dresses, carriage rides to the church, tear-jerker ceremonies and champagne fountains. And then we grow up and realise that our piggy bank savings don't stretch quite as far as our eight-year-old imagination. But still, with some careful planning and economical groundwork you can achieve, or at least come close to, your fairytale fantasy.

Blank cheque
Start with a wish list. Believe your budget is limitless, that your lotto numbers have just come in and that you can have whatever your heart's desire. Write it down, in all its superfluous glory. Arrival by helicopter, walking down the aisle to the crooning of Michael Bublé, the Pope conducting the ceremony, and a hundred snowy white doves being set free into the sparkling sunlight to mark your love and commitment. You now have your starting point – well, you have to start somewhere. Look at it, discuss it together, put stars beside the things you really want, and question marks besides the ones you could live without. And then turn it over and place it to one side.

Now look at your financial state. What do you want to spend? What can you afford to spend? I'm not going to lie to you — weddings can be expensive. There are of course ways and means of doing things economically, but even with strict monitoring and penny-pinching tactics, your wedding will still cost above and beyond what you expect, and more so, what the groom will expect. By now you will have chosen your wedding date and so will know how long you have to save, earn more money or take out a loan.

Setting the budget

When you initially sit down and set your budget, it is important for you both to decide whether this is the ultimate, maximum amount you can afford to or want to spend, or if it is a figure to which you will try to keep as close to as possible. Most budgets increase throughout the course of planning. Various factors contribute to this: family or friends offer money as a gift or want to contribute; you find suppliers or vendors are more expensive than you thought; you may not have considered a certain aspect that is now important; the bride has fallen in love with her dream dress that is 2k over budget … believe me, it's very easy to get lost in the moment and in continuous spending.

At this point I will say this: brides beware. It seems to be the case that most grooms have no grasp of the cost of wedding-related supplies, requirements or expenses. And feigned heart attacks are par for the course with them during the wedding planning stage. As with most purchases, unless it's electrical, car or sport-related, men rarely see the reason behind spending huge amounts of money on it, and never is this truer than when planning a wedding. You may have to use womanly charm and feminine guile, and maybe a little blackmail, in order to get certain things approved …

Suppliers and money

You only need mention the word 'wedding' and florists, photographers and hotels start to salivate at the prospect of a cash bonanza. It's fair to say that the poor bride and groom are made even poorer by some unscrupulous suppliers and vendors in the wedding market. But of course there are two sides to every coin, and in addition to money-hungry hunters, there are an equal number of budget-friendly buddies. Do be careful though: there is well-documented research into suppliers deliberately overpricing once the word 'wedding' is mentioned. An example of this was demonstrated in a radio call to a florist. A researcher had costed a bouquet of flowers that she wished to have made as a gift. Minutes later her colleague phoned the same florist and had priced the exact same bouquet but mentioned it was to be the bridal bouquet. There was €90 difference in the price. Shocking you may think, but it does happen.

Don't get too frightened though. An affordable wedding is achievable, despite all this. There are numerous publications dedicated to the art of achieving the 'champagne wedding on a Buck's Fizz budget'. And you can, if you put your mind to it, achieve all you want within the confines of your available budget. It's all a question of compromise and good old bargain hunting.

Bearing the costs

So you now know that weddings potentially mean big money, or at the very least a substantial sum. But who pays for what? Nowadays this is all a question of who can pay for what and what people can afford. Traditionally speaking, the costs of a wedding are broken down as shown opposite.

It is rather common now for the bride and groom to pay for everything, or for each set of parents to contribute a sum of money rather than paying for specific items. It is only polite that if parents contribute large sums of money, they have greater say in the guest list and arrangements. Some parents will consider this a God-given right once you have cashed their cheque, so do bear this in mind before accepting any generous offers, or, like me, you could end up with eight flowergirls and four page boys.

Who will bear what costs is something that needs to be decided from the start, and family and bridal party members should be informed of what, if anything, they have to pay for (this could be a decisive factor in them accepting the position ... weddings are not just expensive for the discerning bride and groom!)

Bride

* *Wedding ring for the groom*
* *Wedding gift for the groom*
* *Gifts for the bridal attendants*

Groom

* *The bride's engagement and wedding ring*
* *Wedding gift for the bride*
* *Gifts for the best man and ushers*
* *Groom's wedding attire*
* *Bride's bouquet*
* *Mothers' corsages*
* *Boutonnières for attendants and fathers*
* *Marriage registration fees*
* *Priest or register's fees*
* *The honeymoon*
* *Stag night, unless being paid for by best man*

Bride's Family

* *Engagement party, if one is being held*
* *Ceremony costs: location, music and all other related expenses*
* *Reception costs: food, beverages, entertainment, decoration, wedding cake*
* *Bride's wedding dress and accessories*
* *A gift for the couple*
* *Wedding invitations, announcements and mailing costs*
* *Bridesmaid bouquet*
* *Transportation for bridal party from bride's home to ceremony*
* *Photography/Videography*
* *Floral decorations*

Groom's Family

* *Rehearsal dinner party*
* *A gift for the couple*

Attendants

* *Wedding attire for themselves*
* *Any travel expenses*
* *Wedding gift*
* *Bridal showers, hen party or stag do*

Bride and Groom

* *Gifts for their parents, attendants and anyone else who helped in the planning.*

What can we expect to pay?

So now armed with who and what and where all floating around in your head, I am sure you're beginning to question the cost of things and how much you can be expected to pay. As getting married is something most of us do only once, the majority of us know little of what things cost or what is considered the average. The *Evening Herald* recently conducted a survey and concluded that the average Irish wedding was costing €27,000 in 2007 (you may want to resuscitate the groom at this point).

For the purposes of convenience and to give you an idea of what you can expect to pay in the relative areas, let us assume that your wedding budget is €27,000. Most weddings generally contain the same ingredients, and based on these, here is a budget breakdown of what you can expect to pay:

BUDGET AMOUNT		€27,000
Reception	35%	€9,450
Honeymoon	18%	€4,860
Rings	8%	€2,160
Wedding Dress	6%	€1,620
Flowers	5%	€1,350
Photography	5%	€1,350
Accessories	4%	€1,080
Groom's Wear	3%	€810
Bridesmaids	2%	€540
Transport	2%	€540
Video	2%	€540
Wedding Cake	2%	€540
Fees	2%	€540
Invitations	2%	€540
Miscellaneous	4%	€1,080

So based on the law of averages, these are the suggested amounts someone on a €27,000 budget should expect to pay. I stress the word *suggested!* The amounts you spend or should spend on the various wedding elements will be solely based on your wedding wishes, your priorities and your choices. (Appendix IV, pp. 183–191 details some very useful (and slightly scary!) forms that you can use to keep track of costs and spending.)

Now to take the most expensive element, the reception, and just see how the costings are calculated. The number of guests you invite, for example, will have a huge impact on your budget distribution. Inviting eighty guests on the above budget will allow for huge scope on extras and frills, whereas if you intend on having two hundred guests, the majority of your budget will go on the reception.

In order to calculate what different numbers will cost you, the best thing to do is choose a rough menu and see what it will cost per head, then take multiples of fifty and calculate your rough meal bill (e.g. based on the basic meal calculated in Chapter 13 of €43.25, and a bottle of wine at €20, €10 per person, based on 2.5 glasses each, your approx. per head amount is €53.25):

50 guests	@ €53.25	€2,662.25
100 guests	@ €53.25	€5,325.00
150 guests	@ €53.25	€7,987.50
200 guests	@ €53.25	€10,650.00
250 guests	@ €53.25	€13,312.50

This will give you a rough guide as to how costs will evolve, and bear in mind that this is just for the meal and wine; it does not include a toast, favours or any other extras. (Based on your calculations you should be able to roughly determine the number of guests you can afford to invite; remember that your maximum quoted will be determine by what your venue can cater for.)

Purse strings

There are few of us who are in the lucky position of having a limitless budget, and because of that I have listed some ideas on how you can save money.

* *Hire a planner: with the added bonus of professional advice they will have agreed reductions with suppliers and vendors.*
* *Get married 'out of season' – generally considered October to April – and choose a date that falls midweek.*
* *Limit your number of guests to the reception meal and perhaps invite more to the Afters; a buffet costs little in comparison to a five-course meal for everyone.*
* *Rent or borrow the bridal attire, or purchase from a reputable discount shop.*
* *Instead of hiring transport for the day, ask a friend or family member with a nice car to drive you.*
* *Involve your family and friends as much as and where you can. Budding florists, bakers and beauticians could be in your midst without you realising it.*
* *Opposed to the traditional store gift lists, ask guests to contribute towards the cost of the photographer or band, or simply ask for cash gifts only. While this may offend some guests, others will be thrilled at the prospect of not having to search through department stores for the prefect wedding gift and will be happy in the knowledge that they are giving you something you want.*

Be realistic in your budget and what you can afford. People understand the cost involved in starting a life together, and so don't feel pressured into having a big wedding if you know it's something you can't afford. Friends and family can be very understanding if you explain that you simply cannot afford to invite everyone. You must be honest with each other, decide what the important aspects of the day are for you both and concentrate your budget there.

Remember ...

brides: this is the groom's day also. You should consider his feelings and desires for the day and not just your own, and while him arriving in the A-Team van was not what you envisaged, it may be what he always wanted (and besides, you could always use it as a bargaining tool!)

— 7 —

Location, Location, Location

Where is it all going to take place?

L OCATION SAYS IT all! As with buying a house, choosing the location for your wedding ceremony and reception will say a lot about your wedding, will reflect on your theme and budget, and will set the stage for your big day.

Your first decision: do you marry in Ireland or do you marry abroad? There are obvious pros and cons to each. Marrying in Ireland gives you greater control, but may lead to a larger wedding and potentially a greater spend. Marrying aboard means you may have to leave things to chance due to few visits, potentially have to deal with a language barrier and could be without some of the important people who are not prepared or can't afford to travel.

In this chapter we will make the assumption that you have chosen to marry in Ireland, and while the chapter will be geared in this way, the information can still be adapted and applied if you are considering marrying abroad. For those already decided on a destination wedding, the next chapter details all the pros and cons to a foreign wedding.

The wedding ceremony

As mentioned earlier in Chapter 3, with the reform in the marriage laws, which came into effect in November 2007, it is now possible for your wedding ceremony to take place in a pre-approved building other than a church or registry office, provided the venue has been inspected and approved by the HSE in advance of the marriage ceremony and subject to a registrar being available to solemnise the marriage at that venue on the date in question. Therein lies your second decision. Do you hold your ceremony in a church, registry office or pre-approved building?

CHURCH WEDDING

For any good Irish Catholic girl, a white wedding involves a church. This is traditionally the bride's family church. However, in modern Ireland and with families moving around more frequently, you may have had many family churches, or none at all. Some but not all priests will allow non-parish members to use their church to hold their ceremony once they meet the religious and legal requirements, and for a small fee. Failing this, you could marry in your former university or college church or chapel, or return to a childhood church of which either one of you were fond.

Traditionally a marriage ceremony takes place in the bride's home parish, but it is not unheard of or uncommon for it to happen in the groom's parish or at the church that either set of parents wed in. Nowadays, with many couples setting up home together long before wedding bells sound, it might be a nice idea to marry in your new parish – this would act as a real starting point to you beginning your new lives together.

REGISTRY OFFICE WEDDING

For the non-religious, up until November 2007 the registry office was the only alternative, and usually when people think of a registry office they think of a boring, grey, lifeless building with little character, where the ceremony is preformed in record time, and with little opportunity for nice photos. This is not always the case and there are some charming locations dotted around the country. Registry office ceremonies do tend to involve the bare essentials and normally only accommodate immediate family and friends as the rooms tend to be quite small.

Pre-approved building wedding

Your third option is the 'pre-approved building'. This must be a fixed structure, large enough to accommodate you, your wedding party, all your invited guests, seated, and for the ceremony to take place comfortably. Hotel conference or banqueting rooms, or stately homes with large libraries or conservatories lend themselves to this nicely. Such places are now even advertising their accommodation of these services.

Where you hold your ceremony should be of importance and meaning to you both. With this said, it may be necessary to take into account the feelings of your families as well. Some parents may hear of nothing but their child marrying in a church. It is important, however, that you both are happy with your choice.

Key things to remember when choosing your ceremony location are as follows:

* *It is possible for your service to take place there.*
* *It and your officiant are available on your chosen date.*
* *It will comfortably hold all your invited guests.*
* *It is easily accessible to you and your guests.*
* *It is, at most, a forty-five-minute drive from your reception location.*

Remember ...
It is important that the distance between the location of your ceremony and your reception is as little as possible. Guests will not be best pleased at having to drive an hour or more to the reception and then having to wait around before their meal while photos are taken. Also, time spent travelling will take away from the momentum of your big day!

The reception

Once you have chosen where the ceremony is to take place, you must now turn your attention to the reception. Your reception is without a doubt where you will spend the largest portion of your budget and therefore normally gets the greatest amount of consideration. Where you hold your reception will be influenced by:

❋ *Where it is you are getting married*
❋ *What is available*
❋ *The time of year*
❋ *The type of wedding you want*
❋ *The number of guests being invited*
❋ *The budget you have to spend.*

It really is important to bear in mind that the number of guests you invite will have a huge impact on where you can hold your reception. You may have always dreamt of a stately home or idyllic castle, but unless your guest list is somewhere between eighty and 130, this may not be possible. Many of these incredible settings are small and intimate and not suited for large weddings. A way around this is to hire a marquee for the garden and hold the reception in the grounds. Some may think this a bit of a waste though, as you may be forced to hire the entire house or castle for one or two days and then have the expense of a marquee on top.

As with most aspects of planning a wedding, one of the key things here is to consider your requirements and draw up a wish list. Research thoroughly what is available in your chosen area and what is available in your guest and budget range. Indeed, your options for your reception are limited only by your guest list, budget and imagination. With the vast choice in venue hire, you are sure to find the perfect location that reflects both your sense of style and you as a couple but doesn't damage the budget too much! Here is a list of possible locations:

❋ *Hotel*
❋ *Stately home*
❋ *Country castle*
❋ *Private club*
❋ *Community centre*
❋ *Museum*
❋ *Art gallery*
❋ *Public beach or park*

❋ *Racetrack*
❋ *Bed & Breakfast*
❋ *Yacht or boat*
❋ *Your home or a friend's home.*

Before you get carried away with a gorgeous romantic location or hip new hotel, be sure to investigate any restrictions they may impose. These may include:

❋ *Time restrictions*
❋ *No smoking or candlelight*
❋ *No red wine*
❋ *No floor-damaging stilettos*
❋ *Noise level restrictions*
❋ *No flowers likely to cause pollen stains*
❋ *Age limitations on guests i.e. no children*
❋ *No non-residents in the hotel bar once the reception bar has closed*
❋ *Only being able to purchase wine from the venue opposed to bringing in your own and paying corkage.*

Inspection of venues

Unless, of course, you have your picture-perfect place already picked out, the only way to find the illustrious venue is to get out and start looking, or cruising the net! Once you have made a choice, or at the very least a short list, an inspection is vital. It's important that you both go on these inspections and it is not a bad idea for a parent or member of the wedding party to tag along too. After all, you will be day-dreaming of yourself sashaying through their marbled floored hallway and cutting your five-tier wedding cake with a jewel-encrusted sword and so may not notice potential problems!

I've included a form listing the questions you'll need to ask and the particulars you'll need to get from your venue coordinator in Appendix IV, p. 192–197.

Remember ...

While most hotels offer their 'venue hire' as complimentary, some do charge a hire charge for bank holiday
weekends or key calendar dates. Be sure to clarify this
during your inspection. And while some places (hotels)
may not charge for their main banqueting hall, they may
charge for additional rooms for drinks receptions, kids
corners etc. Be sure on every charge to get a true picture of
your costs, and if the information is not volunteered, ask!
Don't find out when you go to pay the bill that it's a few
more grand than what you had expected.

— 8 —

Destination Weddings

Marriage in the sun

ABOUT HALF-WAY THROUGH OUR ENGAGEMENT, during our own hair-pulling and door-slamming phase, my future mother-in-law suggested we elope and marry abroad. In the same breath she also stated that, if we did, she wouldn't be coming! (An innate fear of flying being the reason, not the prospect of her eldest son marrying me.) It seemed rather appealing at the time, but I knew it wasn't for us. I always wanted the big, lavish, traditional white wedding, and I knew that if I didn't do it this time around, I never would (of course not suggesting that I plan to get married again!)

A destination wedding involves the bride and groom and a party of twenty+ travelling abroad to a foreign destination for a week or two, during which the bride and groom get married. It's generally small and intimate, cost-effective for the bride and groom and has the added bonus of combining both the marriage and honeymoon in one. A wedding abroad makes for a unique occasion all round, from the flowers and favours to the location and, of course, your wedding ceremony itself. All the various ingredients will be a mix of your own personal style and traditions and those of your chosen destination, making your wedding experience truly memorable. If climate is an issue, a wedding abroad is likely to be a much safer bet. And depending on where you choose to go, thanks to all the low-cost travel options now available, a destination wedding does not have to cost the earth!

Why marry abroad?
While not an option everyone will consider, the popularity of destination weddings has definitely been on the rise over the past few years. Low budget airlines and the internet have made the world a much smaller and more affordable place. And so, popping across to France or Cyprus to make a lifelong commitment in front of your nearest and dearest is nearly cheaper than inviting 200 guests to a five-course meal in the local four star hotel. Whether your idyllic dream includes the rustic Tuscan countryside or the white sandy beaches and tropical waters of the Seychelles, there is endless choice and scope out there to satisfy any and all tastes.

Besides the obvious guaranteed weather (unless you are considering Alaska or Greenland), there are a number of other reasons couples choose this way of getting married:

* *Place or family of origin*
* *Budget*
* *Less hassle and fuss*
* *Avail of local or alternative cultures or traditions*
* *A lifelong dream*
* *A desire to travel*
* *A smaller, more intimate wedding.*

But while picturesque ceremony locations filled with happy, tanned couples may smile back at you from the tour operator's brochure, a destination wedding still takes planning, research and time, and it may not turn out to be quite the easy option you had hoped for.

Planning for a wedding abroad

Planning a destination wedding is made slightly more difficult by the possible language barrier and time difference if you have chosen a long-haul location. There are three main ways in which you can approach a destination wedding:

> ✳ *The DIY option*
> ✳ *Booking a package through a tour operator*
> ✳ *Using a wedding planner.*

Where to go?

Regardless of the option you choose, research is essential! Probably the best place to begin with is your destination. This in itself is a minefield! The current destination wedding hotspots include:

> ✳ *Italy*
> ✳ *Mauritius*
> ✳ *Dubrovnik*
> ✳ *Cyprus*
> ✳ *Austria*
> ✳ *Las Vegas*
> ✳ *South Africa*
> ✳ *France*
> ✳ *Malta.*

Normally when a couple are deciding where and when to go, they look at what the destination has to offer them in terms of weather, scenery, culture and activities. They want options for where the ceremony might take place: small stone chapels in the countryside, historical venues in town and castles, villas or countryside manors for their reception. They want a destination that offers a host of possibilities, somewhere that is rich in history and culture, with a convivial lifestyle, resulting in the perfect setting for them and their guests.

Remember ...

Do be careful of the indentikit destination wedding packages that have been springing up in some of the more popular destinations. With thousands of Irish now travelling abroad to say 'I do', many hotels and planners have jumped on board, and 'uniquely tailored packages' may not be as 'individual' as you had hoped.

As with contracting any service, before you make a decision on whether you will approach your wedding in the DIY, tour operator or planner way, get quotes and details of services provided for your various options. Consider the amount of time you have to put into researching a wedding abroad, and the extra money long-distance phone calls and research trips will cost you. Finding a planner or tour operator who has a partner or office in Ireland with whom you can deal may make the whole process more personable and enjoyable, and there is a certain amount of reassurance and accountability in being able to call into their offices. You do have the added bonus that nothing will get 'lost in translation' either. This is a service we offer in conjunction with partners based on location in key wedding destination hotspots around the world.

One of the major drawbacks to planning a destination wedding is the limited visits to your chosen locations or the fact that you may not get to meet your chosen suppliers or vendors until the day of the wedding. Few couples get the chance to pop over and back as often as they would like during the planning stage and often have to rely heavily on second-hand or third-hand experience, advice and recommendations, brochures and photographs. Because of this limited access, and to avoid disappointment or disaster when you arrive, it is vitally important that you heed the following two points:

RESEARCH

I cannot stress this enough. Regardless of whether you have chosen the DIY route, are using a tour operator or have hired a wedding planner, research is key! Be sure you are 100 per cent happy and trust the method and choices you have made. Not only are you relying on yourself or your hired help to make the happiest day of your life happen, you are also trusting them with your honeymoon and the welfare and happiness of your twenty nearest and dearest. Be sure that the advice and recommendations you are getting are right; just because you have hired someone to do the work for you, it takes nothing to post a topic on a forum and get some feedback … it may save you huge heartache later.

PLAN AND KEEP PEOPLE INFORMED

As they say, if you fail to plan, you plan to fail! Organising a wedding is a military operation – people need to know what they are doing and when. Normally this just involves your immediate family and wedding party, but with a destination wedding this now involves all guests who are attending. The quickest, cheapest and easiest way to keep everyone informed is online.

Creating a wedding website of your own is the easiest and often cheapist way of letting everyone know flight, accommodation and transport details etc. Having a dedicated wedding email address will mean that suppliers, vendors and guests can keep in touch with you and you will have all information in one place. For those guests who do not have access to email, the fact that all the information is compiled and sorted means you can easily print off the information for them and post it out. Appoint a bridesmaid or groomsman to update those without internet access to make sure guests know about any changes that may occur in the course of your planning.

Having discussed the various destination wedding aspects with our partners abroad, we always strongly advise that couples use a wedding planner or agent to help them during their preparation. Getting married is no simple task, and the choice of a destination wedding only adds to the research and time needed to plan this mammoth operation. As far as the tour operator is concerened, this is not their core business, and couples need to know that they are receiving the personal touch, that everything will run as smoothly as it would if they were at home. The only way to ensure this is by working with a wedding planner and, better still, one based at home and at the destination – this is definitely the winning combination.

Requirements for marriage abroad

To have a legally binding marriage, you must adhere to the marriage laws of the country you wish to wed in, while also meeting the requirements to marry under Irish law to make your marriage valid in Ireland (revert back to Chapter 3, p. 31 for information on these requirements). Each country and/or religion will have their own requirements and you may find it useful to employ the services of an agent or planner to prepare and file these papers and to translate any special requirements you may have to adhere to. In some countries you will be asked to provide a Certificate of Freedom to Marry, also known as the *Certificate de Coutume* or *Certificate of Nulla Osta*. This certification is issued by the Department of Foreign Affairs and states that you are not already married and are free to marry. To apply, if living in Ireland, contact:

> Consular Section
> Department of Foreign Affairs
> 72–76 St Stephen's Green
> Dublin 2
> Tel: 01 4082568
> Web: www.dfa.ie

If living abroad, contact your nearest Irish embassy. The certificate will then be posted out to you (except in the case that you are marrying in Rome, in which case the certificate will be sent directly to the Irish Embassy in Rome and then forwarded to the relevant district). On receipt of your certificate, you can then forward it to your wedding planner or agent to be processed in the correct way. In addition to this certificate, you will also need a copy of your birth certificate, most likely the long version, and a valid ten-year passport that has at least six months left on it from your *date of return* to Ireland or your home place following the marriage. Do also check with your tour operator/travel agent or airport about any other aspects of the travel criteria you may need to follow.

Think about your guests
Do consider your guests when making your choices. As happy as they may be to follow you around the world and be present for your special day, think of them when choosing your destination, time of year and travel plans. Keep flight times as short as possible so that guests can just go for a few days if they don't have the holidays or spending money to spare or have made other plans themselves. Choose a time of year that will benefit from good weather but be mild enough so as not to be uncomfortable. Also, a time of year that is just out of season will mean that rates are more reasonable and that resorts or hotels will not be packed.

Don't be offended if key people you thought would come can't attend. You've decided to marry abroad, and it may be that some friends and family can't afford to travel, or travelling is too much for them because they are old or infirm or because circumstance has commited them elsewhere. Remember, in choosing to marry outside Ireland you run a much higher risk of key people being unable to attend your wedding. This is something you will have to deal with graciously and will be perhaps one of your main considerations when choosing whether to marry at home or abroad.

Hair, make-up and attire
Most likely you will not have the chance to have hair and make-up trials before your big day. And unless you have the budget to fly your own personal hair and make-up team out with you, or are lucky enough to have some professionals lurking amongst your family and friends, you will either be at the mercy and talents of a local professional or you'll be doing it yourself. If this is the case, prepare yourself! Most women wear make-up every single day of their lives, yet few know how to apply it correctly. Take a course! From a ten-week evening course in the local school to one-on-one lessons in the beauty salon to a full-on professional course in a city centre academy, there are plenty of options

available to you. It is something you will use for evermore and it will give you peace of mind knowing that you don't have to worry about how you will look on the day.

What not to wear

Regardless of the wedding location, most brides will still consider and want a traditional wedding dress. Arriving onto sandy shores or into sweltering heat, they quickly realise their mistake! Before you start dress shopping, consider where and when your wedding is going to take place. If marrying on or close to sand, consider the potential damage this can cause to a detailed or lacy dress. While most brides choose to marry during hopefully warm weather at home in Ireland, this is nothing compared to the summer weather enjoyed abroad, and while you can happily wear a layered and heavy dress during an Irish summer, to wear the same in the Italian heat may cause you to tire easily and become dehydrated, not to mention the discomfort of sitting in a hot, sticky, sweaty dress all day. Buy a dress that is suitable for your wedding location, or have a second lighter and less formal dress that you can change into.

Arrive early

Regardless of how carefully you've planned, and the hard work of your tour operator or planner (if you have used one), arriving a week or a few days in advance of your wedding day will give you a chance to double-check all arrangements and have a proper run through everything. If during this you realise that something is not going to work, or you have forgotten or left behind a key item, there is still time to sort the matter.

Pricing and budget

As I have already mentioned, one of the key reasons couples decide to have a destination wedding is down to budget. As much as they may have liked to have had the big family wedding at home, it may just have been cost-prohibitive, and so in choosing to go abroad for the big day they are hoping (in a way!) that not all invited will be able to attend. Or often they only invite immediate family and friends. As with all wedding budgets, the cost of a destination wedding really depends on where you choose to go and what you choose to pay. The average spend seems to range from €8,000–€12,000, which includes:

❋ *Flights and two weeks' accommodation for the bride and groom*
❋ *Ceremony fees and a reception for forty to 100 guests*
❋ *Wedding attire for the bridal party*
❋ *Photographer*
❋ *Videographer*
❋ *Flowers*
❋ *Invitations*
❋ *Ceremony and reception music and entertainment*
❋ *Transportation (although in most cases this is not required).*

Some couples, if only having a small wedding of about twenty, choose to pay for flights and accommodation for their guests. Again this will come as a package, and in doing so they are generally still saving compared to a big family affair at home. Regardless of what way you decide to do things, it's important that you make it clear to those invited. For a wedding at home, invites are normally sent six to eight weeks in advance of the wedding day. For a destination wedding, these would want to be going out at least six to eight *months* in advance; earlier, if all details and rates have been confirmed. The more time you give guests to save and secure days off, the likelier they are to attend. When sending out your invites, tell guests the costs of flights, accommodation, booking details and booking dates. Be as thorough as possible – this will cut down on the number of questions people need to ask. In having a destination wedding, you will become your guests' unofficial travel agent. If you are not prepared for this, or don't have the time, arrange with your tour operator or planner for guests to deal directly with them, or appoint a member of your wedding party as tour director (though clear it with them first!)

Although a destination wedding does pose many challenges and obstacles, so does any wedding, regardless of its location. If you have properly researched and planned, anything is possible. Take time to consider your options, and do discuss them amongst yourselves and with your family … don't set your hearts on it, only to find out that your parents won't travel!

— SECTION THREE —
The Art of Wedding Management

— 9 —

The Wedding Planner

What are the benefits of having a professional involved?

FOR MOST COUPLES, planning a wedding is an emotional, highly strung, joyous event. They take approximately 253 hours to plan and are currently costing on average €27,000–€33,000. Planning for such an event will inevitably lead to fights among couples and families ... don't worry, these all (normally) get resolved and all the hard work combines to result in one magical day!

Being a wedding planner, I am bound by my own company law to always promote and advise positively on hiring a wedding professional! Especially one from my own company! In all seriousness though, this is a choice that you and your intended should make in the early stages of your own negotiations. Planning a wedding is an amazing, stressful, time-consuming, head-wrecking experience. You will both love and hate every moment and having an extra pair of professional hands can be a huge help.

When I started Distinctive Weddings I was clear that our aim was to provide couples with a realistic, professional service from which they would benefit. Having seen weddings from all sides, both as a bride and as a planner, I know how invaluable it is to have a professional involved in arranging and executing a wedding.

There are several reasons I might advise having a planner:

* *Professional, realistic advice is second to none. Mum's, Dad's, Aunt Imelda's advice is all well and good, but they cannot and will not have all the information – merely a good idea about things. You need someone who really knows what they are doing, and, more importantly, is going to do it the way you want! You are paying for a service to get what you want, not what the father-in-law thinks you want!*
* *Having someone who is not emotionally involved in the experience and who can be impartial in their advice and suggestions will help resolve issues and aid in situations where compromise is needed quickly.*
* *Time ... I plan weddings for a living. I am not a teacher, doctor, bricklayer or secretary having to plan a wedding in the evenings; I do it full time. Planning a wedding takes weeks, months and sometimes years ... details, research, sourcing, meetings, negotiating, all take time, something which working professionals with family, social and work commitments have little of to spare.*
* *Budgeting! During the course of your engagement, you will think that your husband-to-be has become a parrot trained to say 'How much does it cost?' – my own adopted this condition in the first week! One of the most important things for brides and grooms when planning is keeping to the budget and not overspending. Having a professional who is able to keep an eye on this area is invaluable! Established planners will have discounts in place with various suppliers and vendors which they should pass on to clients.*
* *People in the business know other people in the business, and because of this they know who is good, what is value for money, as well as some of the tricks of the trade.*
* *Planners remove stress. Or at least they're supposed to! Weddings are stressful, especially for the bride. Having someone to hand the reins to on the day gives you an amazing sense of relief and leaves you to enjoy the day thoroughly.*

It's a common misapprehension that wedding planners are only used by or affordable to the rich and famous. This is not the case, of all, at least.

Couples must take into consideration the services being provided and the work being carried out. A wedding planner can work from anything from a couple of hours to months planning your wedding. Not only are you paying them for their time, but also for the resources they have access to and their knowledge and expertise. You could pay a wedding band the same amount of money for two to three hours of their time that you would pay a planner for several days, weeks, or even months of work.

When it comes to pricing, there are really no industry guidelines. There are actually very few wedding planners per population, or wedding for that matter, in Ireland. Generally, cost is largely dependent on the package and tasks being covered. A general rule of thumb is to expect to pay somewhere in the region of 10 per cent of your budget for a complete planning package and in the region of €250–€1,200 for a full day coordination. Hourly rates run from €50–€250 depending on companies and tasks.

PACKAGES EXPLAINED
For your convenience, planners will often have a number of tailored packages for you to choose from. These will give you an indication of the services they offer and the level of detail they can go into. As most couples' requirements are unique, the planner will often create a bespoke package that caters specifically to their needs, wants and (where possible) budget.

Packages normally include some of the following:

* *Complete planning, co-ordination and design (normally priced in gold, silver and bronze options, depending on budget and size of the wedding)*
* *Decor packages that help you design and achieve that wow wedding*
* *On-the-day packages that help co-ordinate and bring together all the details you have worked so hard on over the months.*

Remember ...

A good planner should not take over your wedding. In essence they are there to aid, assist and advise you. You must feel 100 per cent comfortable with them and trust them completely, or the relationship will not work. When considering hiring a planner, chat with a few over the phone. Get a feel for who they are and what they are like. Some will offer a free first consultation: avail of this. Meet them in person, discuss ideas and then decide if they are right for you.

— 10 —

Paper Mates

Deciding on the guest list and issuing invites

WEDDING STATIONERY is the collective name given to 'Save the Date' cards, invitations, RSVP cards, Mass booklets, menu cards, place names and 'Thank You' cards. They generally all follow the same theme or colour and reflect the style of the wedding. You have numerous options in pre-made store or internet bought, DIY, custom made, emails, simple letters etc.

The guest list

Before any wedding stationery is ordered, you will first need to decide on guest numbers. This in itself is a minefield, made easier perhaps if you and your intended are footing the entire bill. If a set or both sets of parents are contributing, it is only fair they have a greater say in who is and is not invited. When Hubby and I were planning our wedding, we originally wanted an average-sized wedding of approximately 150 guests. Both coming from large families and having numerous close friends, this actually rose to 285 invites. You'll be surprised how quickly numbers add up. Of course, we included all the kiddies, partners and most of our work colleagues, so we didn't do ourselves any favours!

Once you have a rough idea as to the number you intend to invite, make a list of your VIPs – this should include all members of the wedding party. They are often overlooked as you know they are going to be there, but they do contribute to your overall numbers. Once you have outlined those who have priority, see the numbers you have left. No doubt your VIPs will include some of the people either set of parents will have on their list also. At this point then, provided you still have room to spare, it is time to see who the in-laws and the outlaws wish to add. You have the option of asking them to compile a list and see what they come up with – it may not be as bad as you thought and you may be easily able to accommodate everyone. Your other alternative is to give them each a number, say forty guests each (and in the interest of democracy, best to give them both the same amount – after all, marriage is for life and family grudges can last forever!) If either don't use their full quota you can then pass the surplus on to the other. If you find it difficult to keep numbers down, consider your options:

* *Have a 'no children' policy, or only invite immediate family members. Whichever you decide, make sure it is the same for both families so as not to cause offence. Traditionally, all aged above sixteen years receive their own invite, so you can use this as one cut-off point; the other obvious one is eighteen years.*
* *No partners: most cousins, some aunts and uncles, and a few friends will no doubt have other halves whom you don't know or haven't met … are you prepared to pay for a meal and drinks for people you don't know? Chances are everyone invited will know at least three or four other people at the wedding so it is not like they will be flying solo!*
* *Only invite aunts and uncles and the first-born cousins, or no cousins at all. This can be a tricky one – it works better if you perhaps come from a large family or one that is not particularly close. Weddings are notorious for causing pre-existing problems to boil over, and the family guest list is always a good one for getting the water bubbling. It may have nothing to do with you, and you may not even be involved, but a lot of noses can be put out of joint when an invite isn't issued.*

❋ *Most of us work in large offices with numerous 'colleagues',*
some of whom we dislike sharing a stapler with, never mind
our wedding day. However, we must remember office politics:
inviting immediate managers and those in superior positions
is a good career move, and often they will not attend. But don't
go to the extreme of inviting the entire board of directors, unless,
of course, you know them and they you personally … it may be
considered a bit over the top. Following that, your immediate
work colleagues and work friends are next in line. As for the
remaining drones, well, that's what the Afters are for! That
way they get to see you looking fabulous, but you don't have
the added problem of trying to airbrush them out of the
majority of your wedding photos!

With invites you can safely assume that somewhere from 15 to 20 per cent of those invited will not come. This will be due to a combination of prior commitments, being unable to travel, sickness etc. Of the 285 we invited, we had 190 to the meal, and that was eight below the final number we had given to the hotel forty-eight hours previously. I should probably say at this point that the maximum number of guests our venue could cater for was 240, and they had advised that a maximum of 220 would be more than comfortable … so, as you can imagine, I was a little apprehensive for a while!

'Save the Date'
'Save the Date' cards generally take the format of business cards, although some companies offer the facility of making them into fridge magnets, postcards, cups etc., which can include pictures and images. They need only be simple in layout and format, and generally comprise of the following:

SAVE THE DATE

8th of August 2008

For the Marriage of
Anne Walker to Patrick Dunne

Invitation will follow

As these are sent out a year or so in advance of the wedding, long before you may have decided on the colour, theme or style, it may be an idea to keep them as simple as possible. You may find an email or blank card works just as well. Many good stationery shops now sell pre-cut business cards in printable formats, and with a good home printer you can easily do them yourself. This is what I did and they turned out to be most effective.

Formal invites

Following the 'Save the Date' cards, the next piece of wedding-related correspondence your guests will receive from you is the invitation. Normally, wedding invites are sent out six to eight weeks in advance of the wedding date with the RSVP date being no later than ten to fourteen days before the wedding. As I've mentioned already in Chapter 7, if you are marrying abroad, you may want to think about sending your invites out six to eight months in advance with your RSVP date one to two months before your wedding. This is to give you and all your guests plenty of time to save and prepare. You can, of course, alter these time frames as you see fit, but bear in mind that the less time you give guests, the less likely they are to be available, and the closer your RSVP date is to the wedding date, the less time you have to ring around and chase those stragglers. Just because someone has not RSVPd, do not assume they are not coming. Unless you have received an RSVP card, phone call, fax or email saying they *aren't* coming, assume they are and double-check to be sure.

Designing the invites

As with all the wedding-related stationery, your options, between professionally designed and DIY, are endless. Professionally or custom-made invites generally come in complete matching packages and all you need provide are the names, addresses, locations, dates and times and the rest is done for you. They range in price from €300–€1,500, depending on choices, finishes and quantities. They can be purchased mail order, online or through a stationery store. Pre-made invites also come in matching sets or you can pick 'n' mix between those available. All you need add here are names, dates, locations and times. They sometimes work out as the cheaper option and you can always investigate discounts if bulk-buying. A useful form listing questions to ask your stationery agent is given at the back in Appendix IV, p. 201.

I favour the DIY option, possibly because I have been designing and making invites and cards since I was about fourteen. If you have the time and patience, you can let your creative juices flow. It is also a nice way for you both to spend time together while still getting along with the wedding preparations.

Bear in mind: designing, making and producing your own invites takes time, patience and can be *very* frustrating! It is not something for the faint of heart or short of temper. Most stationery, craft or bookshops sell all the paraphernalia you will need and there are endless online or Ebay stores selling supplies at fantastic value. A good easy-to-use printer is a must, or alternatively you can have them professionally printed (though this may boost your costs).

It is important to remember that you will only need one invite per couple, on which you can include '& kids', or their names, provided they are under sixteen years. When ordering or making, it's always best to order/make an extra ten or so, as doubtlessly there will be that last-minute one you forgot about or a spelling mistake or two somewhere.

Top Tip!
Regardless of who or how your invites are being made or printed, proofreading before going to print is a must! It is always a good idea to ask a 'fresh' pair of eyes to do this for you, someone who has not been involved in the design or layout and who is possibly better placed to be vigilant. Grammatical errors or spelling mistakes will look sloppy, and it would be a shame to send something out that has mistakes in it after you've gone to all that trouble and expense.

It's only words

The wording of an invite is dependent on the family circumstances of the bride and groom and/or who is paying for the big day. As the bride's parents traditionally pay for the wedding, the invites would be sent from them to each guest. However, over the years this has evolved and changed and there are now numerous options to choose from based on your circumstances. Following now are examples that you can use depending on your circumstances:

TRADITIONAL INVITATION

MR. & MRS. JOHN WALKER
Request the pleasure of your company
at the marriage of their daughter

Anne Marie
to
Mr. Patrick Thomas Dunne

Friday, 8th of August 2008
at 2pm

in the Church of the Immaculate Conception
Ashbourne, Co. Meath

COMBINED CEREMONY AND RECEPTION INVITATION
This also includes the RSVP at the bottom. Some couples include a separate RSVP card as well, or a designated email or voice service.

Mr. & Mrs. John Walker
Request the pleasure of your company
at the marriage of their daughter

Anne Marie
to
Mr. Patrick Thomas Dunne

Friday, 8th of August 2008
at 2pm

in the Church of the Immaculate Conception
Ashbourne, Co. Meath

With the Reception to follow at
The Ashbourne House Hotel, Ashbourne, Co. Meath

RSVP   July 25th 2008

1 Highfield Drive   Phone: 01 1234567
Ashbourne, Co. Meath   Email: wedding@gmail.com

A REMARRIED MOTHER HOSTS
A remarried mother will use her new husband's name but state
the daughter as hers rather than theirs.

Mr. & Mrs. David Cummins
Request the pleasure of your company
at the marriage of her daughter

Anne Marie
to
Mr. Patrick Thomas Dunne

Friday, 8th of August 2008
at 2pm

in the Church of the Immaculate Conception
Ashbourne, Co. Meath

With the Reception to follow at
The Ashbourne House Hotel, Ashbourne, Co. Meath

RSVP   July 25th 2008

1 Highfield Drive   Phone: 01 1234567
Ashbourne, Co. Meath   Email: wedding@gmail.com

A REMARRIED FATHER HOSTS

MR. & MRS. JOHN WALKER
Request the pleasure of your company
at the marriage of his daughter

ONE DIVORCED UNMARRIED PARENT HOSTS

When the bride's unmarried mother hosts she uses her maiden
and her married name.

MR. & MRS. KATHLEEN JONES WALKER
Request the pleasure of your company
at the marriage of her daughter

Anne Marie

to

Mr. Patrick Thomas Dunne

Friday, 8th of August 2008
at 2pm

in the Church of the Immaculate Conception
Ashbourne, Co. Meath

With the Reception to follow at
The Ashbourne House Hotel, Ashbourne, Co. Meath

RSVP   July 25th 2008

1 Highfield Drive   Phone: 01 1234567
Ashbourne, Co. Meath   Email: wedding@gmail.com

WHEN THE BRIDE'S UNMARRIED FATHER HOSTS

MR. JOHN WALKER
Requests the pleasure of your company
at the marriage of his daughter

If the bride's parents are divorced and both remarried but wish to co-host the wedding, the mother of the bride's name should appear first.

MR. & MRS. DAVID CUMMINS
and
MR. & MRS. JOHN WALKER
Request the pleasure of your
company at the marriage of

Anne Marie
to
Mr. Patrick Thomas Dunne

Friday, 8th of August 2008
at 2pm

in the Church of the Immaculate Conception
Ashbourne, Co. Meath

With the Reception to follow at
The Ashbourne House Hotel, Ashbourne, Co. Meath

RSVP   July 25th 2008

1 Highfield Drive   Phone: 01 1234567
Ashbourne, Co. Meath   Email: wedding@gmail.com

A STEPMOTHER HOSTS

In the event that the stepmother has raised the bride, or the bride's mother is deceased, the wedding invite can read as follows:

MR. & MRS. JOHN WALKER
Request the pleasure of your company
at the marriage of Mrs. Walker's stepdaughter

DIVORCED UNMARRIED PARENTS AS CO-HOSTS
This can be used in the event that the bride's parents are divorced
and neither have remarried.

MRS. KATHLEEN JONES WALKER
and
MR. JOHN WALKER
Request the pleasure of your company
at the marriage of their daughter

Anne Marie
to
Mr. Patrick Thomas Dunne

Friday, 8th of August 2008
at 2pm

in the Church of the Immaculate Conception
Ashbourne, Co. Meath

With the Reception to follow at
The Ashbourne House Hotel, Ashbourne, Co. Meath

RSVP   July 25th 2008

1 Highfield Drive   Phone: 01 1234567
Ashbourne, Co. Meath   Email: wedding@gmail.com

An informal option to this invite is to delete the Mr. and Mrs.

KATHLEEN JONES WALKER
and
JOHN WALKER
Request the pleasure of your company
at the marriage of their daughter

Depending on the relationship between the divorced parents you
could also consider the more traditional invite as per the first
example. You may want to check with them first that they are both
comfortable with this.

MR. & MRS. JAMES DUNNE
Request the pleasure of your
company at the marriage of

Anne Marie
to their son
Patrick Thomas Dunne

Friday, 8th of August 2008
at 2pm

in the Church of the Immaculate Conception
Ashbourne, Co. Meath

With the Reception to follow at
The Ashbourne House Hotel, Ashbourne, Co. Meath

RSVP   July 25th 2008

1 Highfield Drive   Phone: 01 1234567
Ashbourne, Co. Meath   Email: wedding@gmail.com

BRIDE'S AND GROOM'S PARENTS CO-HOST

MR. & MRS. JOHN WALKER
and
MR. & MRS. JAMES DUNNE
Request the pleasure of your company
at the marriage of their children

Anne Marie
to
Patrick Thomas Dunne

The pleasure of your company
is requested at the marriage of

Anne Marie

to

Patrick Thomas Dunne

Friday, 8th of August 2008
at 2pm

in the Church of the Immaculate Conception
Ashbourne, Co. Meath

With the Reception to follow at
The Ashbourne House Hotel, Ashbourne, Co. Meath

RSVP   July 25th 2008

1 Highfield Drive   Phone: 01 1234567
Ashbourne, Co. Meath   Email: wedding@gmail.com

INFORMAL WORDING — BRIDE'S PARENTS HOST

We ask only those dearest to us to join us in the pleasure of
celebrating the marriage of our daughter Anne to Patrick Dunne

Friday, 8th of August 2008
at 2pm

in the Church of the Immaculate Conception
Ashbourne, Co. Meath

With the Reception to follow at
The Ashbourne House Hotel, Ashbourne, Co. Meath

RSVP   July 25th 2008

1 Highfield Drive   Phone: 01 1234567
Ashbourne, Co. Meath   Email: wedding@gmail.com

We invite you to join us in celebrating our love.
On this day we will marry the one we
laugh with, live for, dream with and love.
We have chosen to continue our growth through marriage.

Please join

Anne Marie
and
Patrick Thomas Dunne

Friday, 8th of August 2008
at 2pm

in the Church of the Immaculate Conception
Ashbourne, Co. Meath

With the Reception to follow at
The Ashbourne House Hotel, Ashbourne, Co. Meath

RSVP   July 25th 2008

1 Highfield Drive   Phone: 01 1234567
Ashbourne, Co. Meath   Email: wedding@gmail.com

Children inviting guests to the marriage of their parents

Sarah and Michael Walker
and
Sophie, Declan and Josh Cummins
Request the pleasure of your company
at the marriage of their parents

Kathleen Jones Walker
to
David Cummins

*The pleasure of your company
is requested at the reaffirmation of
the wedding vows of*

Mr. & Mrs. John Walker

*in the Church of the Immaculate Conception
Ashbourne, Co. Meath*

*With the Reception to follow at
The Ashbourne House Hotel, Ashbourne, Co. Meath*

RSVP   July 25th 2008

1 Highfield Drive   Phone: 01 1234567
Ashbourne, Co. Meath   Email: wedding@gmail.com

RSVP

Accompanying your invites you may decide to include an RSVP card. This is an easy way for guests to inform you of their intention to attend or not, if they remember to post them that is! Some couples decide to have these pre-stamped to encourage guests to return them – this can be a costly and sometimes fruitless exercise.

They are normally about postcard sized, are pre-addressed and look something like this:

The favour of your reply is requested
by the 25th July 2008

....

Will be able to attend [ ]   Will not be able to attend [ ]

Please indicate if you have any special dietary requirements

....

You will see also that RSVP cards can be used to find out about any vegetarian or special dietary requirements.

Again to keep costs to a minimum, if you decide to have RSVP cards, they are something you can easily design and print yourselves, or include them as part of your wedding stationery package.

> **Top Tip!**
> It is a good idea to number each RSVP card and note this number down in a spreadsheet along with each guest's name; no doubt one or two will forget to add their names to them and this will rectify this.

Including helpful info

In addition to RSVP cards, couples now increasingly see the need to include directions, a list of local accommodation and a list of local amenities and/or activities. With families being spread more and more apart, weddings often become a mini family holiday and so the need to provide more information has slowly increased. Some couples have websites designed for this very reason and there are numerous free online facilities that can cater for this. Other alternatives include creating a little booklet that accompanies your invite or printing a few pages up and including it. Another way of letting guests know about different aspects associated with the wedding and the area is including a 'Wedding A to Z'. You may find that putting a little bit of extra work into this when sending your invites out will be much appreciated by travelling guests and reduce the number of calls and questions you will receive. It's a fun and easy way of passing on relevant information to guests – mine got a big kick out of it, and I've included it on p. 211 to give you an idea.

The Mass booklet

Once you have your invitations all sorted, the next job requiring your attention is the Mass booklet. As I've said earlier, couples tend to forget the importance of the ceremony and Mass. Most of the emphasis of a wedding day is placed on the reception and couples often just throw a booklet together, allowing the priest or a parent to choose the readings. Your wedding ceremony will be one of the most moving and touching ceremonies you partake in. Spending the time going through all your different reading, prayer and hymn choices together and making the occasion something unique to you is very important and will make the ceremony very special.

Your priest or celebrant will be able to advise on the appropriate readings, prayers and hymns for your ceremony or Mass. As I've mentioned before in Chapter 2, a superb way of compiling the booklet yourself is by using *www.gettingmarried.ie*. A recently launched site, it brings you through each aspect of a marriage ceremony, detailing all the appropriate readings and prayers for each part of the Mass. It allows you to easily build, save and edit your booklet and then print once complete.

Another popular option is to use a combination of booklets kept from over the years from other ceremonies. I tend to discourage this myself – they are not always correct in their layout, literature or format and often contain numerous errors. But I have included a sample Mass booklet at the back in Appendix III to give you a flavour of what it might look like.

When producing your booklet I always advise that two different versions are made. The first I call the master copy – this should contain all aspects of the Mass or ceremony: names, details etc., and should be used by the priest, bride and groom, plus a copy for the ambo (the priest's lectern) and one for the musicians, and a spare in case anyone loses theirs. The second copy is the public copy. This should be the 'watered down', shorter version of the master. It is not necessary to give the guests every reading, hymn or prayer in full – few will read it, and printing up and stapling together hundreds of pages is costly and time consuming. Mass booklets are used for the hour to hour-and-half of your ceremony. Some bring them home as a memento of the day and the remainder are thrown away. Despite this, I do advise that you have Mass booklets or cards. It reaffirms to you both the importance of the day, it focuses guests' attentions during the ceremony and it is always nice to see your vows in print! A popular and easy variation of the Mass booklet is the Mass scroll. This is simply an A4 sheet, possibly coloured, with your Mass printed on it and rolled and tied with a ribbon. It is simple, easy and also extremely cost effective.

In terms of quantity, it is not necessary to print a booklet for every guest – couples and friends can share and so I always advise to print one booklet for every two guests. Booklets can be handed out by your ushers or groomsmen as they greet guests, left in a basket or on a table in the entrance hallway or scattered along the pews.

Seating arrangements and place names

Numbering tables can often cause offence as Auntie Mary may not like her position all the way at the back at Table 20! But naming your tables can continue your theme and avoid the shame of being seated down the list. Using colours, movie titles or band names, months of the year or Disney characters are but a few options. Often hotels and venues print both table plans and table names; all you need do is provide the details.

In addition to seating plans, you can if you wish tell your guests exactly where to sit by using place name cards. These are optional, and few venues provide them, but they can easily be purchased online or from any stationery store. Having them professionally scribed by a calligrapher can be expensive, so having them printed with your other stationery may work out cheaper. Alternatively, you can buy a nice pen and have a go yourself!

Top Tip!
Always buy a few extra items of stationery to cover the inevitable mistakes and forgotten guests!

Most venues supply personalised menu cards that are placed on each table and perhaps in the drinks reception area – this will be stated in your package and will include your names, marriage date and the meal you have chosen. You will have little control over these – they generally take a preformatted layout using the hotel's own colours. You can if you wish go to the expense of having your own printed to match your other stationery, but this money could perhaps be put to better use elsewhere. If this is something you are keen on doing you could also investigate fun alternatives – having them printed on edible paper, made up in chocolate, or if you are sparing no expense, carved as ice sculptures!

Saying 'thanks'

A dying art is the 'Thank You' card. Most, if not all, guests will give a gift of some description and you may even receive some from people who are not even invited. Saying thank you is not only polite but will be greatly appreciated. It wasn't until I started sending my own cards out that I realised that couples rarely did it anymore. I was actually getting 'Thank You' cards in reply! Again your choices, as with the invites, are many and varied. A nice idea is to send a photo of the bride and groom with the card, or to have this as the card. Sneaking away for a minute or two on the day with your photographer and a pre-made 'Thank You' sign will be a lovely surprise for your guests with each card.

For gifts received before the wedding (up to two weeks) it is best to send 'Thank You' cards out straight away. This will leave less to do afterwards. Then, following the wedding, 'Thank You' cards should ideally be sent within three to four months. If you are marrying close to Christmas you could send them with your Christmas cards, as it is customary to send a card to each invited guest the year you marry ... after that you can be more selective! This is a great way of cutting down on postage, and although I married in July I stretched my thank yous out to be sent with the Christmas cards (naughty me!)

— 11 —

Cutting a Dash

Dressing the wedding party

I THINK IT STARTS when we're about three — the desire to wear yards and yards of taffeta, lace and silk. We root around in our mother's wardrobes, looking for anything vaguely resembling a ball gown, slip on her highest of heels and pose for photographs in front of the mirror. This goes on with our own dressing-up clothes and the ensembles of our sisters and friends until the day when we get to go shopping for our own wedding dress.

For me, with such dressing up came a hazy idea of a wedding dress, but never a concrete idea of the actual one. Deciding on what works for you only comes from trying on a range of dresses in all different shapes and styles. Few of us are in that lucky position of buying and wearing numerous evening or formal dresses. Indeed, the closest many of us have gotten to wearing such a dress was at our Debs.

Negotiating the various bridal boutiques around the country can be a nightmare. My virginal trip was a bit embarrassing. Just for the sake of it, my chief bridesmaid and I ambled into a boutique in town. The girl behind the counter smiled at us politely as we walked towards the dresses. We casually browsed the rails, mentally selecting what we did and didn't like. I walked in on a bride-to-be trying on a dress (oh, have I class). At this point, a red-faced sales assistant approached (finally, some service!), but before she could say anything, I asked to try on some dresses. She queried if I had an appointment, and when I said 'No', her face turned stony and we were ushered to the front of the shop. On our exit we hastily made an appointment for two weeks' time …

Appointments are key! Without them you will most definitely receive short shrift in the various bridal houses around the country. And you will have heard that a number of boutiques have a reputation for being rude, arrogant, unhelpful and downright ignorant of your needs or wishes. This unfortunately is true of some. You have only to do a search on the various wedding websites to read some first-hand accounts of bedraggled brides. Don't let this put you off! To be forewarned is to be forearmed.

Research

You may be saying to yourself, if I have to make an appointment to try on dresses, how am I supposed to know if they have dresses I want to try on? There are a few ways around this. First, you will need to do a little bit of research yourself. While it's important to leave your final decision on the shape and style of dress you want until you try things on, do look into what you like. Bridal magazines and the internet are great for this. See what you like and print out your favourites if you have the facility. Most bridal shops now have accompanying websites with galleries of some of the styles and a list of the designers they stock. Alternatively, if you have fallen in love with a specific designer or one of their dresses, they will be able to inform you of the nearest stockist to you. If you don't have a specific designer in mind, but have printed off some styles you like, take them with you when you go to make appointments. Call into a few bridal shops and show them the pictures to see if they stock similar dresses and make an appointment based on that.

Heed advice

Regardless of whether you are going to buy your dress from a shop, online, from a friend or have one made, do try them on. As well as the fact that it's loads of fun, it will open your eyes to the styles and shapes available. You may be surprised at what does and doesn't suit you. To my first appointment I brought my mother and my best friend, who was also my chief bridesmaid. I didn't just bring them because of their involvement in the wedding but because I valued and trusted their opinions above anyone else's and I knew they would be brutally honest with me, however harsh the opinion! On arrival at the shop we were told to have a look around and select some dresses that we liked. From our previous trip I had a particular one in mind, and it was just as gorgeous as I had remembered. My mother agreed, as did another shopper, who insisted I try it on. I had butterflies in my tummy ... this was going to be 'the one' – I knew it! When I emerged through the plush red curtains, I had to do a double take in the mirrors, and not in a good way. What stood before me wasn't me, it couldn't be ... it was a hundred-ton pregnant whale surely? The gorgeous gown just looked hideous on me. I was devastated! The next two weren't much better. My happy mood was rapidly fading.

After those three the next dress was one the sales assistant had chosen for me. I didn't like it one little bit! It was everything I did not want in a dress. I refused to try it on but she insisted, and so, to appease her, I did. I was now feeling like an oversized oaf and in no mood for another ten-ton Tessie reflection. But when I saw my reflection in the mirror, I actually let out a gasp! My mother welled up. I looked like a bride! The dress was stunning on me. I would have walked out of the shop there and then and headed straight for the church. It felt right. It looked right. It was right! I did try on another few dresses, but kept returning to that one. So, from my experience, a good sales assistant will know what they are talking about, so listen to them, and even to humour them, do try on a dress or two that they suggest. You may just be surprised!

One thing I will mention, mainly for the larger brides like myself (proud size 16) – most bridal shops, unless specialist, will not have dresses in your size. Most 'stock' dresses that are used for fittings will be a size 12 to 14. They will put a panel of material in the rear (across the bodice) of the dress to close it up. For this reason you must also use your imagination a little as your own dress will fit much better. Another thing, for all brides, wedding dress sizes do not necessarily follow the same sizing scale as clothes, and while you might be a size 10 or 12, you may find that the sales assistant orders you a bigger size for your wedding dress. Don't be alarmed by this – if you find that it is a little big when it does arrive, time permitting, alterations can be made.

Mishapes, mistakes, misfits

As with all clothes, there are some styles that suit certain figures over others. This topic in itself would comprise a whole book, and one I fully recommend is *The Wedding Dress Sourcebook* by Philip Delamore – my wedding dress bible! For those of you looking for a brief outline on various styles, the following should help.

THE BALL GOWN

This is the fairytale princess dress of which we have all dreamed. The fitted bodice, voluminous skirt, petticoats and train, it epitomises everything that is the wedding dress.

The style works well for a number of different figures. Tall and slim brides with broad shoulders may find that a strapless version works best for them, while small-framed brides or those preferring to stay covered up may prefer off-the-shoulder straps or a bolero-style jacket to match. Medium height or pear-shaped brides will find this style great for hiding large hips, and the fuller busted amongst us will be able to distract from the twins (if you so wish!) by emphasising the waist with a corset-style bodice.

PRINCESS LINE

The Princess Line is a favourite cut in women's tailoring because of its clean, minimal and slimming shape. It is often closely associated with the A-Line due to their similar fit and flare; however, a Princess Line is unbroken from top to bottom and divides the dress in vertical panels. These vertical lines are one of the main characteristics of the Princess Line, usually starting from the shoulder, but can curve from the armhole to the hem of the dress.

Floral displays are a quick and easy way to add colour, theme and decoration to your ceremony, whether in a church or elsewhere!

Adding floral details to the backs of your chairs is a great focal point.

Alternative options to the traditional pew ends, all of which can be reused in other aspects of the wedding day decor!

Bouquets of choice!

Alternative options to traditional bouquets!

Splashes of colour in the reception decor.

A rather more extravagent affair!; using colour to full effect; and a neat and minimalist styling scheme.

The traditional white iced, three-tier wedding cake versus the cupcake wedding cake.

Traditional fillings – alternative icing!

Due to the numerous different style options (from mini to shift dress, sheaths to columns, and bell skirts to fishtails and beyond) this cut will suit most body types and heights. While it works particularly well on tall curvy types, it can also offer the illusion of curves on those who have anything but! It can re-proportion petite brides with long bodies with a high waist and shape and flare to the skirt, and when used with the right underwear can disguise ample hips and bums.

EMPIRE LINE

A style made fashionable during the Regency Period, it embodies all that is 'Sense and Sensibility'. A raised waistline cut beneath the bust gathers to an often-full dress which drops to the floor, giving a marvellous elongated silhouette. The neckline is normally a deep square and finished with either straps cut wide at the shoulder or worn with a cap.

This style again is a good all-rounder. Because of its high waist it covers a multitude of sins. Short legs, long bodies and pear shapes are hidden and small busts are emphasised with the deep square neckline.

MERMAID AND FISHTAIL

Mermaid and Fishtail scream Hollywood glamour! They are for the über slim and glamorous amongst us. The fabric is cut diagonally to the grain, allowing it to drape around the body and is typically figure-hugging to the knee and then flaring to the hem (Mermaid) or collecting in a pool as it hits the floor (Fishtail).

This style is not for the faint-hearted. It requires 'the Body' and the confidence to pull it off. Unless you are comfortable going commando, this is probably not the dress for you. VPLs and straps are a common mistake with these styles and totally distract from the overall effect.

A-Line

This is possibly one of the best known, after the Ball Gown, and is another great all-rounder. As the name suggests, this is a fitted top or bodice with a full skirt and a horizontal seam across the waist – one of its main differences from the similar Empire Line. The A-Line will suit those wishing to have a short mini to the full floor-length skirt.

It has much the same properties as the Empire Line, elongating a short frame and emphasising the waist on curvaceous figures. One of its many forms is sure to suit all once the proportion to your body is right.

The Column

Think tall and slim. This style issues a simple yet striking statement. It is understated in its design and comes either as a deconstructed 1920s short skirt or as a long, lean 1950s constructed form. The style can help to control or disguise a figure but is best suited to the taller and more proportioned amongst us. Though it can work for tall and curvy brides, if you have a bust or rely on a bra it is probably best to steer clear of this style. While it works extremely well for tall people, it would not be my first choice for a slimmer bride, unless the dress is waisted.

Mini, Midi or Suit

Perhaps in the minority when choosing a bridal outfit, and something some brides would never even consider, are the Mini, Midi or Suit Option. A Mini or Midi, falling just above or below the knee, may be considered by those marrying aboard, marrying for the second time or for those brides who would never normally wear a dress. These styles are generally suited to the slimmer and more athletic amongst us, particularly so of the Mini, while our curvy cousins can glide down the aisle in the Midi. Some brides are ingenious enough to have a full-length skirt for the ceremony which transforms to the Mini or Midi for the reception.

A Suit can at times be a little controversial, especially for the more mature or conservative amongst your guests. Regardless of your figure you will be able to find a Suit that flatters you. Wearing a Suit is more a statement of your personality and your sense of style, but as with a dress, it will be the cut and finish that will deem suitability and flatter the figure, so again it's important to try on a few different styles.

There is no one main stockist for the Wedding Suit; it is truly a bespoke item. A bridal boutique may not stock 'the Wedding Suit' but may know of a designer of theirs who includes one in a collection. Your best bet will most likely be Brown Thomas, Debenhams or Clery's, where you may be able to find an 'off the peg' suit which would be appropriate. Failing that, find an excellent tailor. This is probably your best option: it will be down to your choice of fabric and your style of design, and you will be assured of having a truly unique wedding outfit!

Bridal underwear

Some of you will think I am mad when I say this, but your underwear is possibly more important than your dress as regards the overall look. That is, underwear is the foundation of the whole thing, and if the foundation isn't right, the ensemble falls down!

The type of dress you choose will obviously have an impact on the underwear you select. Once the dress is chosen, ask the dressmaker for advice on the best style and type of underwear you should buy to accompany it.

Once you know what you should be looking for, start looking! Don't leave it too late. Ideally you should have your underwear bought and collected (in the case of it being made to order) before your dress fittings.

Bear in mind that functionality and comfort should come before anything else when choosing your underwear. You will wear this from the morning of your wedding day right through to the early hours of the following day. You want it to look and feel right all the time, while giving you the comfort and support you need. It also gives you a real chance to find something extra special to knock his socks off on the wedding night!

Buying the dress

But back to the dress! Once you have found it you now need to decide: shop bought, designer creation, dressmakers, online, borrowed or second-hand. When ordering from a shop, designer or dressmaker, you really need to put in your order *at least* six months before the wedding. This is to allow for your dress to be made, altered and for you to have it in your possession somewhere in the region of four to six weeks prior to the day. Most shops or designers will not be able to guarantee your dress in time for your wedding if you leave it any shorter than this.

It is a growing trend for brides to find their dresses in a boutique and then source the same dress online for cheaper. This is a definite possibility. However, do be careful as to the sites you use. Research the reputation of the site from whom you intend to buy and ask for feedback from previous purchasers. This is a definite way of saving money in this area as long as you remember the mantra, 'buyer beware'.

Despite finding the perfect dress that day, in the end I went down the dressmaker route. It had long been my mother's dream to make my wedding dress, and while I was skeptical at first, it definitely turned out to be 'the one'! Loosely based on the dress I had tried on and with my wedding dress bible in hand, I designed my own. We bought the fabric in Hickey's for €453. The dressmaking process was a dream because of my mum's involvement, and dress fittings and alterations could happen every other day. I was in the lucky position of not having to pay for 'labour' when my dress was being made, as this can be considerable. Dress making may not be the money-saving option you had hoped for, unless you are trying to replicate a dress that is way outside your budget. In this case it can end up being very economical.

What to spend?

I am often asked what a bride should spend on her wedding dress. There is no hard and fast rule on this; it is entirely up to the bride. Dresses can start from as little as €100 second-hand or from a charity shop and go on into the thousands for a designer creation. On average you're looking at something from €700–€4,000.

Remember ...

The price you are given during your dress fittings may not be the actual price you pay. Some shops, not all, do add additional charges, such as fitting fees, designer alteration fees or a variety of other expenses. Do ask before leaving if there are any additional charges, and if they say there are not, get them to sign and date the quotation to this effect. Sometimes these 'incidental charges' can add another €1,000–€2,000 to the dress.

The shoes

To talk for a minute about wedding shoes, this is something brides always forget to consider when choosing a style or length of dress. I was shopping for some bridal shoes a few weeks back and went into a favourite haunt of mine off Grafton Street that always proves fruitful. It's a small place, and while browsing I couldn't help but overhear a conversation a bride-to-be was having with the sales assistant. The bride, who was a decent 5'9", had been all over Dublin looking for 5" bridal shoes ... the assistant informed her that they didn't stock such a height and few bridal shoes came in that heel. She showed her other designs in 3.5" and 4". The bride became hysterical, saying that it had to be 5" – she had had her dress fitting in 5" heels and nothing else would do. A cardinal mistake! Going through the entire day in 5" heels could only be, I'd imagine, a nightmare! The recommended heel height for a bride is 1"–3.5" and even at that you will find you will remove your shoes towards the end of the night. Remember, the height of the shoe you wear to a fitting will influence the length of your skirt and you *must* remember this when you buy your bridal shoes!

Top tips for dress shopping

☀ *Make appointments.*

☀ *Bring with you people whose opinions your trust and value. As my own best friend Aoife says, if your friends say that you look like Nelly the elephant's larger cousin, you do. You need to take opinionated types with you ... you don't want Ellie immortalised in wedding photographs.*

☀ *Don't put on any fake tan beforehand, and wear only a little bit of make-up, if any at all, and none on your chest.*

☀ *Bring make-up removal wipes and tissues with you. Some shops ask you to remove all your make-up before trying on any dress.*

☀ *Also bring deodorant – by the time you're finished you'll be sweating! Only use it though when you are changing back into your own clothes and the dresses have been removed from the fitting rooms. You don't want to stain or damage anything!*

☀ *Wear good, plain underwear – fussy lace, frills and details will make it harder for the dress to sit naturally on you. Make sure they are white or nude – don't wear black! A good fitted bra is important if you are considering a strapless dress, but if you don't have a good bodice or strapless bra, wear a good bra of your own to see the shape of the dress first and then hide the straps for an overall impression. If you've bought your bridal lingerie already, wear it!*

☀ *Wear your hair so that you can put it up and take it down easily, so as to get an idea of how you might wear it with each dress. Ask the shop assistant to recommend tiaras/veils etc. that might suit the dress – this will help you decide what works best with your hair style and colour.*

☀ *If you have one, bring a digital camera, but clear it with the bridal shop or designer first. Photographs will help refresh your memory if you don't decide there and then which to order.*

☀ *This may sound obvious, but have a good breakfast or lunch before you go in ... I've had a few fainters who want to feel slim trying on dresses and so don't eat, and then this coupled with all the changing and the heat proves too much.*

☀ *As I've said, choose a height of heel from 1"–3.5" for your bridal shoe and consider this when fitting and trying on a dress. If you have bought your shoes, bring them with you and wear them during the fitting. If you haven't, most shops will have pairs that you can use; in this case, bring pop socks with you.*

☀ *Try on dress styles you might not normally consider and listen to the advice of the sales assistant – some do actually know what they are talking about.*

☀ *Bear in mind that the shop dresses are generally in a size 12 or 14, with some larger 16 or 18, so they may or may not stock in your size. Therefore it's important to remember that your own will be much better fitted. They will fit it on you as best they can to give you a good idea.*

☀ *Most importantly, don't feel pressured into ordering on the day! But do order your dress with plenty of time to spare. Some shops or designers require orders of a minimum six to eight months in advance of your wedding day, or they just turn you away.*

Making an Entrance

Walking, riding, driving or flying

WHEN I WAS younger I was obsessed with Cinderella, and couldn't understand why I didn't have a fairy godmother or why my own mother wouldn't let me keep four mice and a pumpkin just in case. I longed to travel by horse and carriage, but, needless to say, I didn't get much chance during my youth … nothing seemed to rise to the occasion! And so, once he popped the question, I knew my chance had arrived. For me it was the ultimate in fairytale fantasy – and if you can't be a princess on your wedding day, when can you be?

Organising transport

Now, while transport to and from the wedding is the place to really push the boat out (literally, in some cases), it also requires a very practical side that many overlook. You need to organise the transport for the wedding party. This includes the bride and groom, both sets of parents, bridesmaids and groomsmen and flowergirls and page boys. It is not necessary to *hire* transport, but it is important that you make sure they have a way of getting around and that they know about it. Traditionally, the bride and her father travel to the church together. They are normally preceded or followed by the bride's mother, bridesmaids and flowergirls. The best man normally takes the groom and the groom's parents and the other groomsmen bring themselves.

Here comes the bride – in a DeLorean

How you arrive will be really down to your own taste, style and budget. The traditional choice is the old 1920s- or 40s-style classic car or the more modern limousine. In strong competition with these now are Bentleys, BMWs, Hummers, Mercs, rentals, taxis, helicopters, horse and carriages, and, believe it or not, walking! Again, the choices are endless. For some, this area is only a means to an end, a way of getting from A to B; for others it is the be all and end all!

An important factor to consider when choosing your transport is its possible limitations. For me, it was the distance the horses could travel versus the time it would take them. My parents' house is less than a mile to the church so this was fine. Our reception, however, was eight miles from the church – not a colossal distance, granted, but a considerable distance for two horses and a carriage to travel. To solve this I hired a gorgeous Beauford car, which first took my bridesmaids and mother to the church; they then transferred into some friends' stylish cars and we were away! Perhaps an unnecessary expense in some people's views at €925 and €550 respectively, but I wouldn't change a thing!

Fantasies are what weddings are made of and all should be considered in order to make it a day you will both treasure. Some brides-to-be will gasp a little when their fiancé brings forth a crumpled picture of KITT the car from the famed *Knightrider* series (just praise the Lord it wasn't the A-Team van! And if it was, expect that the chocolate fountain will be agreed to!) The transport arrangements are possibly the one area where your groom will show an interest, so don't shoot him down. It may not go with the overall classical style you had agreed on (had he been listening) but it may make his day.

Transporting the guests

After the wedding party is taken care of, you may wish to organise transport for those who do not drive, or who have travelled from abroad and are not hiring cars. Or you may be extremely generous and arrange transport for most of your guests so that they can enjoy a drink and not worry about getting home. Wedding buses and coaches are ideal in these situations. Buses range in size from ten-seaters upwards, and if you shop around you should be able to get a decent price. Dublin Bus offers a wedding bus hire service in the greater Dublin area that ranges in price from €550–€600 (approximately).

If you have decided to hire transportation for all your guests, it is best to state this in the invite and ask those who wish to avail of it to contact you immediately so you can determine numbers, pick-up points and times. It is a good idea to have two or three central pick-up points for guests to meet the bus at specified times, and then for guests leaving in the evening it is a good idea to have two departure times from the hotel, perhaps at 11.30 p.m. or 12 a.m. and again then once the bar closes and music ends. If you are very generous you could have a third departure time the following day for any guests who may have stayed in the hotel.

As I had eight flowergirls and four page boys, some with non-driving parents, I 'borrowed' a fourteen-seater minibus to ferry them all around. The bus belonged to a local club with whom we are friends and a small donatation was all they asked for in return – they even provided a driver! The bus was not the most modern, but it was clean and functional and did the trick! No one will notice or pay much heed to less-than-perfect areas like this; after all, they will be too busy looking at the stunning bride!

The practicalities

Before paying a deposit or hiring any vehicles, it is important to first check that the company in question is fully licensed and insured. There are many wedding car 'companies' operating illegally, and while the Taxi Regulator has a great success rate in prosecuting such illegal operations, these 'companies' often keep a low profile so as to avoid unwanted attention. Enforcement officers do patrol the wedding fairs and monitor existing companies; this 'big brother' style approach has caused many non-compliant companies to shut up shop, sometimes leaving brides stranded on their way to the altar! Any car company you hire/contract should have Public Service Vehicle (PSV) tests, insurance and licence. You would hope that simply asking them this would suffice, but unfortunately it's too easy to say yes – double-checking is the best way, and this is easy to do through the Taxi Regulator or by checking the details of the Yellow or Silver disc in the vehicle window. Remember, if the car company your hire is not PSV tested, insured and licenced and you have an accident, you are not covered.

At the back in Appendix IV, p. 204, I've listed some of the important questions you'll need to ask any company you consider hiring for transportation.

U&ME4EVR

Once you have the car or carriage picked, and are satisfied that you are fully tested, insured and licensed, you can now turn your attention to personalising it! The majority of car hire companies provide complimentary flowers and ribbon in your chosen colours. To take this one step further, you may consider wedding car plates. These 'registration' plates are lovely mementos of your day. They normally include the bride's and groom's names and the wedding date. They are available from a range of places, from T-shirt print stores to sign writers shops, and range in price from as little as €13–€55 for a pair.

Top Tip!
Because the wedding industry has flourished so much over the past few years, you have only to open a bridal magazine or the Golden Pages to see the vast range available in wedding transportation. The price can also differ greatly. Shop around, ask for discounts … see if they offer any other services you may use to get a better deal.

— 13 —

Feeding Frenzy

Getting the menu right

IT IS SAD TO SAY IT, but the success of a wedding is often judged on the quality and quantity of the meal provided. This is particularly true in the opinion of older generations. Often I've overheard conversations between women discussing recent weddings they have attended: 'Oh Maura, the wedding was just awful! The beef was dry and rubbery; poor Seán couldn't even chew it, and him with the new dentures, and not a decent potato to be had!' 'Mary, I know what you mean. Sure wasn't I at Claire Cumisky's wedding there, and all they served was that "nouveau cuisine" – a teaspoon of peas and carrots with a piece of salmon no bigger than your finger. The whole thing was a disgrace … and we after giving them Waterford Crystal wine glasses, six of them!' Sound familiar?

It is impossible to choose a meal that is going to satisfy everyone, so my advice is, don't. It is important that the meal you have chosen is one that you and your immediate family will enjoy – after that, everyone else who enjoys it is a bonus! There are of course a few foods or meals you can avoid so as to appeal to the broadest number of guests as possible.

❋ *Stay away from heavily spiced or seasoned foods, unless there is a cooler alternative offered.*

❋ *Always provide a vegetarian alternative and any other dietary specific meal if you have been specifically advised or are aware of such. Ensure your venue/caterer can accommodate these well in advance.*

❋ *Avoid shellfish and nuts as these are the two foods that people are most commonly allergic to and which cause the most instantly devastating effects. You don't want your wedding breakfast marred by Aunt Mildred going into anaphylactic shock.*

On arrival at the venue

Most Irish wedding ceremonies start at some point between noon and 3 p.m., so bear in mind that guests will have had an early breakfast to facilitate travelling, and as the ceremony is taking place during lunch time, the next meal they eat will be the wedding breakfast (so called because of the traditional fast the bride and groom would undertake before their wedding, thus breaking the fast with this meal after the marriage ceremony).

It is almost expected that on arrival at the reception venue tea and coffee and perhaps a light snack of scones is served to guests to stave off the hunger while the official photographs are being taken. Not all venues offer this service as complimentary, so it is important that you check the particulars of your package in case you need to arrange this separately. I would strongly recommend asking that this be done if it is not already included; most guests would 'murder a cuppa' at this point and it will leave a bad taste if they have to fork out for it themselves!

Champagne and chocolate fountains

A champagne or Buck's Fizz drinks reception would also normally take place at this point, and depending on the time of year, fruit punch or mulled wine might make a nice alternative. This type of reception is normally always an added extra and is not expected – many couples prefer to save here and spend the money on a toasting drink for their guests during the speeches.

There is a recent growing fashion to accompany the tea and coffee or drinks reception with a chocolate fountain … this is a fun alternative snack to scones and peanuts and goes down well with all age groups! Some hotels have now jumped on this band wagon and are offering it as complimentary or as an added extra, meaning you have one less supplier to source and negotiate with. The cost of chocolate fountain hire will be largely dependent on the size of the fountain and the number ordered, but for the hire of one large fountain, operator, lights, chocolate, fruit and marshmallows for 150 guests, you are probably looking at a cost of around €650, plus €1.50/€2.00 for each additional guest.

In addition to hiring chocolate fountains, it is now possible to hire champagne/cocktail fountains. This is a relatively unique way of having your drinks reception. Similar to the chocolate fountain, price is dependent on the number hired and whether the alcohol is to be provided. Prices for operated fountains with or without alcohol range from about €540–€690 for two hours. It is also possible to just hire the fountain from a Hire All company for in the region of €75 for the weekend; however, you would need someone to operate it. The drinks fountains are rather effective when accompanied by strawberry and/or chocolate trees – small trees fashioned out of strawberries and chocolate truffles placed around your drinks reception for guests to pick at and nibble on. These are priced at about €60–€90 per tree plus delivery, depending on size and supplier.

The main meal – choices, numbers and costs
SEATING PLAN
Within an hour or so of your arrival at the venue, guests are normally called for the meal. Most will be eager to know where and with whom you have seated them for the meal. In the entrance hall or near the dining hall the hotel/venue will have placed the seating plan. You, your intended and no doubt your immediate family will have put hours of sweat and tears into making sure that Aunt Assumpta's estranged husband and his twenty-five-year-old wife are not in sight and that Uncle John is seated as far from the bar as possible, and still you will doubt the success of your layout! Determining where to seat people is hard

work. Trying to match personalities, humours and interests of people who have never met before can be a nightmare and there is no easy solution. Most hotels and venues insist on a seating plan so as to avoid the scramble for seats or frustration when couples or families are inadvertantly held up. My advice when planning who and where to seat people is to mix it up! Two families and two sets of friends are most likely meeting en mass for the first time and asking them to be nice and civil to each other for the duration of a meal is not too much.

When planning our seating arrangements we divided our family and friends in two and sat them with their counterparts, seating couples and singletons with their opposites while ensuring they knew at least one other person at the table. We paired guests with those of similar age, interests or careers and threw in a few red herrings who we knew could cope! With seventeen children at our wedding (who, by the way, made it what it was, much to my surprise) we had two designated child tables in the middle manned by two Montessori teachers. Surrounding the tables we seated all the parents who could keep an eye on their darlings but could enjoy their meal in peace!

MEAL CHOICES
Your options with regard to the type and style of meal you can serve will be defined by the limitations of your chosen venue. A sit-down four- or five-course meal is generally what is served for the wedding breakfast. Normally this comprises of a starter, main course, dessert and tea or coffee served with chocolates or short bread. A fish course and/or sorbet normally makes up the remaining course. While guests will be hungry at this point, it is important to get the balance between sating their hunger and not stuffing them to the point where they resemble bloated sloths, unable to partake in the rest of the evening's entertainment. Most venues and caterers charge per head for the meal, with beverages charged separately. You will generally be asked to provide your final figures within forty-eight hours, possibly sooner, of the day, and this is the minimum amount you will pay. Most venues and caterers will be able to accommodate one or two surprise guests if they turn up, and don't worry, these additions will be added to your final bill!

It is important to be clear on the charges involved. Venues and caterers generally have individual prices for each starter, main course and dessert and will charge an additional €5–€10 (approx.) per course you decide to have a choice in, while others will have a set price per head, offering you a choice in each course. A wedding meal can range in price from €40–€120 per head.

The following meal is based on 2007 pricings of a mid-range Co. Meath Hotel.

STARTER
Sweet Fan of Honeydew Melon   €7.25

SOUP COURSE
Arklow Bay Seafood Chowder   €6.25

MAIN COURSE
Traditional Roast Turkey & Baked Ham
                                          €19.80

DESSERT
Apple & Winterberry Crumble with Fresh Custard
                                          €6.80

Freshly brewed Tea & Coffee with After Dinner Mints
                                          €3.15

This meal will cost €43.25 per head. To add a choice of main course instantly bumps this up to €48.25, as would choices elsewhere. As with most aspects of your wedding, submit your 'dream' menu to the hotel for correct pricing and alter until you are comfortable with the menu choices and price.

Deciding on the menu

A tasting of the menu before you submit your final selection is a must! I would suggest you narrow your choices down to one to three options in each course for your tasting. Be aware that some, but not all, hotels offer the tasting as part of the package; most charge you, like any meal, for the privilege, but either way it's important to do a tasing. A good idea is to invite along either set of parents or the best man and bridesmaid to have alternative input. However, it's best to probably leave it at that; as they say, too many cooks spoil the broth. Each person should order a different course, or have two of each option served to the table. Everyone should taste everything, with attention focusing on appearance, colours, quantity, quality and taste. By the end of it you should be able to eliminate certain courses. Doing out a score card for everyone on what they think is a fun way of eliminating what not to have!

Top Tip!

Children's menus are considerably cheaper, so do not go to the unnecessary expense of serving the main menu to them as it will most likely go uneaten. Sticking to 'in season' produce, chef's specials and hotel specials will keep costs down too.

Booze hounds

During the meal tasting, sample your chosen wines and the house wines. With four at the tasting it will be easy to do this. Unless there's a budding sommelier amongst you, the house wine should be more than sufficient to serve with the meal. It is also a fantastic way of saving – most hotels will have an abundance of house wines and you can negotiate a deal whereby you'll pay for what you open. Requesting wines that the hotel will have to bring in means you'll pay for what you order. Ordering the house wines also works in your favour in the event that your guests drink past what you had predicted – with your permission the hotel can then open additional bottles on your behalf without changing the wine!

If you have always dreamt of boating it over to Le Harve and driving down through the vine-filled wine country of France and stocking up for the big day, best to check first with your venue that they allow you to bring in your own wine, and cost it to ensure that it is actually economical for you. Most hotels and/or venues will charge you €12 (approx.) corkage per bottle opened, while some hotels do not allow 'outside' wine to be served at all. If you have decided that you wish to source and provide your own wine, it is not always necessary to travel abroad. There are numerous companies in Ireland and close by that will deliver direct, and using one of these will at least save you the boat ticket and petrol costs! See p. 161 for some website addresses of such companies.

Remember ...
The corkage charge should be added to the cost of each bottle of wine you have purchased to give you a true indication of the price.

A general rule of thumb when buying wine for your guests is 2–2.5 glasses of wine each. Your hotel will be able to advise on an appropriate number of bottles to purchase and an appropriate number of reserve bottles to hold back in case they are needed. You should get five glasses of wine from a normal-sized bottle so you can use this as the basis for your calculations. The split between red and white wine is sometimes difficult to gauge. An obvious choice is 50/50, but guests aren't always this accom-modating. One of the benefits of purchasing your wine through the hotel is that they will open either as and when required, but when buying in yourself you will need to have decided on the split in advance. Wine is generally only served with the meal, after which guests return to the bar, so there is no need to buy wine for the entire night as it will most likely go unused.

Remember ...

Couples always remember to ensure their guests will have plenty of wine to enjoy throughout the course of their meal, but while water is always present on the table, do give a little consideration to your pioneering guests and those designated drivers. Jugs of cordial for any kids will keep sugar rushes to a minimum and a soft drink alternative for other guests will be much appreciated.

Also, having your wine poured by waiters will ensure that it stretches that bit further, as opposed to being left on the table for guests to help themselves.

One thing to look out for, and a pet hate of mine, is waiters topping up guests' wine glasses when they have only taken a sip. I was at a wedding recently where this was rife. I was a guest and didn't want to cause too much of a fuss, but discretely had a word in the head waiter's ear. At the end of the meal, while the clearing up was taking place, I couldn't control myself and so counted all the remaining filled glasses, which amounted to thirty-three full glasses, some to the brim. I calculated that in the region of ten bottles of wine was about to be thrown down the drain! I always make a point of saying this to hotel staff and keep an eye out for it on the day – no point in pouring away good money!

Open bars

There is not one of us who doesn't love abusing an open bar! Conversations comprising, 'I'm going to drink all around me at the Christmas party and screw them for the pay rise I shoulda got' will no doubt ring true. It is one thing to use and abuse the seeming generosity of a cold-hearted boss, but it's a real eye-opener to see family and friends do the same at a wedding. By all means, if the budget allows it and it is something you would like to do, an open bar will be welcomed by all guests! I do, however, strongly suggest that you set down strict guidelines with the hotel in advance.

* *Single measures only! — A kid in a candy shop springs to mind, and I have seen it where every order is a double, triple or more!*
* *No premium or top-shelf spirits; specify regular brands only.*
* *Set a time limit on the open bar.*
* *Set a monetary limit on the open bar, at which time of breach the hotel staff can advise and see if you wish to increase. Depending on your budget and the time of night, it may or may not be a good idea to continue with it.*
* *Have a specific drink theme to your open bar, as in, all vodka-based cocktails are free etc. Guests can then pay for any alternative drinks they want.*

Don't get too concerned with having an open bar — few people have one. Expense and budget is top priority and the money can be better spent elsewhere. Guests do not expect it, and comments such as 'It's not like they can't afford it' are usually muttered by the cheapskates who wouldn't have one themselves.

Toasting

Another drinks-related area to consider is the toast. The toast takes place before, during or after the meal, so your obvious choice for your toast drinks is your dinner wine, and I would recommend this if you are conducting the speeches during the meal. If you are having your speeches before or after the meal, a round of drinks purchased for the guests by the bride and groom or a set of parents is a lovely touch. As with the open bar, I would again be clear with the hotel staff on the restrictions relating to this, particularly:

* *Single measures only*
* *No premium or top shelf spirits.*

Hiring drinks facilities

If your reception is being held at home, in a marquee or in a venue that does not have a bar licence or facilities, you may have to hire a bar facility. It is possible to hire bar facilities complete with optics and barrels of beer, and with or without staff and with or without alcohol. Knowing how much alcohol to buy in will depend on the length of the evening, the time of year and the alcoholic tendencies of your guests! It's possibly best to make a list of what friends and family normally drink and average out how many drinks people will have during the night. And again, don't forget the teetotallers and kiddies! Minerals are often overlooked as drinks in themselves and couples can get caught short in only buying enough for mixers.

Top Tip!
If you are supplying the drinks yourself and buying bottled water, a cheeky way of keeping costs down is to buy twenty bottles of premium brand water to be put on the tables, and then, once empty, getting the waiters to fill them up from the tap! Guests will never know the difference! Also, it is not necessary to go to the expense of buying sparkling water – few drink it and it wouldn't work as well with the tap-filling trick!

When hunger strikes later
In addition to your sit-down meal, other alternatives are buffets, barbeques and picnics. Generally these work best for smaller weddings, and not all venues can or will accommodate them. Staff have less control over the order of service: they tend to last longer and involve more serving space and a greater clean up. If it is something you would like to include, an evening buffet served at around 11 p.m. or 12 a.m. for evening guests and midnight snackers is always popular, and a barbeque and/or picnic the following day served for guests who stayed overnight is a lovely way to continue the celebrations. With your evening buffet, it is important to remember that you do not need to order food for everyone. The majority of your guests will still be digesting their dinners, so it's safe to order for in the region of 50–75 per cent of the numbers you have. A good mix of hot and cold foods is ideal and will satisfy most cravings at this point. And remember, the buffet snacks will be an additional price per head, separate from the cost of the meal. Prices range from €9.50–€24.50 (approx.) depending on the numbers and types of food ordered.

Top Tip!

Ask the hotel to keep any sandwiches left over from your evening buffet to be served in the residents bar at 2 a.m. or 3 a.m. Believe me, this will be welcomed with open arms by the hardcore party guests! I have gotten clients based on this suggestion alone!

Should you decide on hiring a marquee ...

If at this point you are reading ahead and still trying to decide between hotel, castle, marquee and caterers, you may want to bear the following in mind. Your initial calculations may seem to suggest that hiring a marquee and caterers is the cheaper option. However, bear in mind that in hiring a marquee and having a 'garden event', you will need to hire everything. Flooring, heating, lighting, tables, chairs, plates, glass, cutlery, decoration, toilets, kitchen appliances and utilities – everything, including the kitchen sink! Now, most good marquee hire firms or caterers should be able to provide all these, but I am sure you can see the mounting costs involved. Another area you may also have to look into with marquee hire is obtaining a bar licence for the evening. Once you have actually sourced a good supplier in this area, the actual logistics are not as complicated as you might first think, but the cost may not be as economical as you had hoped for!

As with every chapter, it is important to be prepared and to cover all your bases during the planning stage. Appendix IV, pp. 192–200 lists detailed forms that should cover all the questions you need to ask and all the issues of which you need to be aware.

The wedding cake

And now to look at the cake cutting ceremony that occurs during the reception. The bride is assisted by the groom in the cutting of the cake, a symbolism of their first task as a married couple. They then feed each other with this first piece – symbolic of their commitment to provide for each other. Wedding cakes are now multi-tiered extravaganzas, a far cry from how they started life. In

Roman times, a loaf of barely bread was baked, and on eating a piece the groom then broke the remainder over the bride's head. The breaking of the bread symbolised the breaking of the bride's virginal state and the subsequent dominance the groom now had over her (a tradition that has long since fallen by the wayside – I wonder why!) During medieval times it was common practice to stack small buns in a large pile in front of the bride and groom, and if the couple managed to kiss over this pile they would be blessed with many children. Appearing from the seventeenth century was the bride's pie, filled with sweet breads, a mince pie or a simple mutton pie. The pie's main 'ingredient' was a glass ring and the tradition was that the lady who found the ring would be the next to marry. The bride's pie was replaced in the nineteenth century by a very basic version of our traditional wedding cake.

The wedding cake we are now all familiar with today started life as a simple, single-tiered plum cake, or variation of, a far cry from what it is today! While some couples only have a cake to adhere to tradition, it is still a very strong tradition. The top tier was normally 'saved' for the christening or to be shared on the first anniversary. Traditionally the bride's or groom's mother, or main female relative, would have baked the wedding cake, and many couples are returning to this tradition either to involve their families more or to save on costs. The cost of a wedding cake is largely dependent on the size, the number of tiers and the fillings and decoration. They can be made or ordered from a bakery, your chosen hotel or by a family member or purchased pre-made from a reputable grocery store. Do check with your hotel about any specific requirements they may have in relation to the purchase, delivery or serving of the wedding cake. Some may insist you purchase your cake through them and many will only allow it to be served with the evening buffet. These reasons are sometimes to do with the chef's policies, or as a matter of principal as some chefs will only allow food that has been prepared, cooked and presented by them to be served from their kitchen.

A recent trend in wedding cakes is the 'fake cake', usually comprising iced cardboard and toilet roll holders. A small section of cake is often included at the rear for the bride and groom to cut. My own personal wonder-woman mother baked our wedding cake. I had always wanted a fairytale castle so in addition to baking actual cakes she also tried her hand at the 'fake cake'! It was a two-tiered, six-turreted, ivy-covered masterpiece complete with monogrammed doors! In addition to the 'fake cake' another popular emerging trend is the cupcake wedding cake.

Top Tip!

If a friend or family member is making your cake, but is not an experienced icer, I fully recommend that you send the cake out to be professionally iced by a baker. Cake icing is a form of art and is nowhere near as simple as you might imagine!

Cake 'fillings' have also been evolving over the years. Couples are now opting for sponge, vanilla, chocolate or a combination of fillings as their choices. As with any supplier it's important that you research your options, the costs and their value. Quality, experience and flare are very important in this area. Price-wise, pre-made, shop-bought cakes (size and filling dependant) start from €50–€170. Professionally made cakes start from about €190+. And it costs about €125 to get a cake (two-tiered fruitcake) iced.

— 14 —

Setting the Tone

How to wow with your wedding

W OW WEDDINGS WERE often thought the preserve of the insanely rich and fabulously famous, upon which we mere mortals could only gaze in the pages of *Hello!* and *Ok!* That is not the case anymore. Slowly and rather more surely, couples are beginning to demand more of their big day than just the run-of-the-mill ceremony, nice meal and good band. Entire gospel choirs, orchestras and award-winning artists are now all fair game for the church music, and helicopter rides to the reception through dove-filled skies are not unheard of (though think of the carnage).

Shortly before starting this chapter, I was watching a rather 'interesting' programme on the telly: *America's Tackiest Weddings.* One couple had decided on a hunt-themed wedding. The groom, a hunter by trade, dreamt of wearing his fatigues and saying his vows perched up a tree … the bride, for her own reasons, complied! She married in khaki green combats and boots – and the guests dressed to match. The groom caught and slaughtered the evening's banquet the morning of the wedding and cooked it on a spit once the ceremony was over. But the 'tackiest' by far was a Halloween-themed/fancy dress wedding. The bride, in full

Goth, was walked down the aisle by Donald Duck and the vows were witnessed by a grizzly bear and a French maid.

Choosing your theme

Most weddings have a theme or style to a degree, whether it's colour, season, hobby, destination etc. related. The theme may be very subtle, or totally in your face (as above). For example, the most common and perhaps most understated is a colour theme. This can begin with your invites where a simple bow adornment or font colour can be continued and worked into bridesmaids' dresses, flowers, church, cake and reception decorations. And this can be the case with any theme chosen. Colour themes are often combined with another theme. Take, for instance, a Christmas theme, with your chosen colours perhaps being gold and red. Your centrepieces may be little decorated evergreen trees or covered boxes acting as faux presents.

With considerably more disposable income than our dear parents, we are now in the position to make our wedding day something truly spectacular, and simple themes and styles easily become wow and wonderful. The easiest way of injecting the wow factor is to hire a wedding designer. Different from a wedding planner, a wedding designer is totally focused on the design, theme and decoration aspect of your wedding and will not be involved so much in the how to's and where for's of invitations etc., although the two can be easily combined.

The wow factor in weddings normally means big bucks. Having those extra touches that set a wow wedding apart from any other does cost money, and while it is achievable by most, it may not be affordable by all. There is also a fine line between wow and 'wowzer'! Walking the tight rope between style masterpiece and tacky sensation can be difficult.

You have only to open a wedding or interior design magazine for inspiration, and most stationery, floral and cake companies can make a creation to match whatever you have chosen. Visiting the websites of wedding planners and looking through their galleries will give you ideas from the very simple to the very extravagant.

Visualise the 'wow'!

A wow wedding is best visualised. For a guest it begins at the church … a red carpet lined with manicured trees leads to the door. Candles twinkle among trailing ivy and luxurious taffeta ribbon. Pew ends are finished with jewelled roses and baby's breath and little cherry blossom trees spring up among the rows. The altar has been transformed by draped muslin, and coloured lights set the centre stage for the ceremony. A melodic choir fills the air with gentle music and little girls in tutus shower the aisle in rose petals. Sounds like something straight out of *The Wedding Planner* movie … but that is what the wow wedding is all about – it oozes theatrical dramatics and movie moment splendour. Perhaps not the wedding for the shy and reserved but definitely the wedding with impact.

There are perhaps four main aspects to achieving such a wedding: flowers, lighting, material and decoration.

Flowers

Gone are the days when a florist merely sticks a ribbon around some wild flowers and sends you down the aisle with a daisy in your hair! Florists create architectural masterpieces, tying a room or theme up in one masterful flick of the wrist. They alone can create a setting that will stun and shock the most seasoned of guests. Using a florist in every aspect of your wedding can definitely create the wow factor. Bringing them along to both ceremony and reception locations will get the creative juices flowing and will give them a greater idea of the impact you want. Floral budgets can range from anywhere between €500 and €6,000 and beyond. In this instance, you really get what you pay for.

Beyond bouquets and buttonholes, couples can sometimes forget where else flowers are generally 'required'. Within churches flowers are respectfully kept to the places in which they would normally appear, just perhaps on a much larger scale. Generally this is because a number of churches require that all floral arrangements used during your ceremony be left behind – by way of a small gesture of thanks to the parish for the use of its church. Because of this, some brides will choose to keep the church flowers simple. If you are unsure as to whether you are required to leave your flowers behind, check with the parish office or the church's flower committee – it might make you re-think your €6,000 flower budget! If you are not required to leave them behind, consider re-using them in the reception decor. This will give you two looks for the price of one!

Before going along to meet with a florist, have a general idea as to what you would like, or at the very least what you would not like! You are not going to be expected to arrive in with a list of flowers, or to place an order immediately. This process takes place over time (or at least it should!) Bring along pictures of bouquets and arrangements you like, samples of material of your chosen colours and a photo of your wedding dress. This will allow the florist to see the style and colour scheme you have chosen, and the style of the dress will give her huge insight into the types of flowers that would suit your day. Be clear on want you don't want but do keep an open mind for suggestions; florists are professionals, they know what flowers work best with what and how to get the best out of arrangements.

In-season flowers

Be aware of what is available and when. Flowers, as I am sure you well know, are seasonal items and while modern growing techniques allow almost anything to be grown regardless of the time of year, buying 'in season' is always best and cheapest!

Spring Flowers include: Anemones, Bluebells, Camellias, Crocuses, Forget-me-nots, Grape Hyacinths, Hyacinths, Lilies of the Valley, Narcissi, Pansies, Ranunculuses, Tupils, Voilets.

Summer Flowers include: Campanulas, Cornflowers, Delphiniums, Hydrangeas, Gypsophila, Jasmine, Lady's Mantle, Larkspurs, Marguerites, Peonies, Phlox, Roses, Scabious, Stocks, Sweet Peas.

Autumn Flowers include: Amaranthus, Chrysanthemums, Cosmos, Dahlias, Hydrangeas, Japanese Anemones, Michaelmas Daisies, Sacbious.

Winter Flowers include: Heather, Hellebores, Irises, Primulas, Snowdrops, Winter Jasmine.

I often find that many mothers of the bride or indeed mothers of the groom want to be involved with the flower arranging. This is sometimes a great idea, or sometimes a really bad idea. You may view flower arranging as a relatively easy task, but believe me, it's not! Much skill, knowledge and expertise goes into even what appear to be the simplest of bouquets. When we are approached by a parent or family member who wants to be involved, we always advise that the bride have her bouquets, buttonholes and corsages made by professionals, but suggest that the mothers, aunties and sisters decorate the church as they see fit. At least in this way we know that the flowers that will appear in most of the pictures will not fall apart! Most florists will be gracious enough to sell on flowers and greenery for whatever arrangements the family may be planning. Other items such as oases, florist wire, tape, cutters etc. will be available from good garden shops.

Alternatively you can also purchase from a flower market – the most popular of these being in Smithfield, Dublin. Normal trading hours are between about 6 a.m. and 11 a.m., so the early bird definitely catches the worm in this case! These traders will take an order in advance, and normally an order is placed in bunches/lots. You will need to determine the type and quantity of flowers required and they will specify the 'lots' in which they are purchased. This can be from as little as 'in 5s' upwards (normally increasing in fives). If you do decide to go down this route there are a few things to consider. Your order could arrive in anywhere from a week to three days before the wedding. The buds/flower heads will generally be closed on arrival and will need time to open in advance of the big day, and so you will need somewhere cool to store all the flowers. *Do not* be tempted to store them in the fridge. You will also need to allow plenty of time to 'make' your arrangements. If you are concerned with a flower's 'shelf life', consider using some of the longer lasting ones. These include: chrysanthemums, carnations, orchids, roses, tulips and calla lilies. Sweet pea and poppy anemones, though beautiful, wither quickly once cut. Also be aware that garden-grown flowers may not last as long as commercially grown flowers and they should always be allowed to stand in water before use. Once your arrangements are made, continually spray with water to keep them fresh and the oasis moist.

Lighting

We are all well aware of the impact lighting can have on a room or event. Low light combined with candles creates a soft, intimate feeling, while stark fluorescents are harsh and clinical. Coloured lights used with draped fabric is an effective way of changing the mood or look in a room and can help with the transition from day to evening if you would like your theme to evolve during the night. Colour gel lights can be hired for approximately €30 per light, and, positioned carefully around the room, can add huge dramatic value.

Most venues will have understood the importance of lighting when the room was designed, and some may even have the provision of hidden additional lighting, so when viewing, do ask about this. Obviously during the meal the lighting will be required to be functional as people will need to see and admire what they are eating! And the majority of venues will complement this 'functional lighting' with some softer accent lighting, most likely by way of candles. If these are not provided they can be easily hired/bought in. A few venues do not allow naked flames, either due to the building's historical/architectural significance or simply insurance reasons – do double-check this. If you are bringing in additional lighting either by way of spot or gel lights, hurricane vases, LED candles etc. do check with your venue's coordinator that there are suitable sockets, voltage and space for them.

Material

Draped fabric and hung muslin can hide a multitude of sins, from an unsightly area of the church to bad plastering on a hotel wall. A dining room can be transformed with tablecloths, chair covers and sashes. Folded napkins can add colour, depth and interest to a table arrangement. Fairy light backdrops and sweeping curtains can frame the top table and later the band on the stage. The possibilities are truly endless and this is really an area in which you can 'go to town'. But be very wary of prices in these areas; they can differ greatly and cheaper is definitely not better in this case!

Chair covers have become almost a wedding staple at this stage, with many hotels and venues offering them as a complimentary feature of venue hire. There are numerous companies who also offer them for hire and their prices differ hugely; they range from €3.50–€6.50 per chair. In reality you should expect to pay in the region of about €4.75–€5.50 per cover (for a standard finish) with sash. Anything below this and you really should be questioning their quality, cleaning and ironing methods.

In addition to chair covers, many companies are now also offering matching tablecloths or runners to complement your scheme. These are approximately €15–€20 each. A sheer or organza overlay added on top of the venue's own tablecloth is an easy way to introduce colour to the room. If this is something you are going for, be sure to advise the venue and arrange with them as to when these would need to be set up so that sufficient time is given over to the task.

A real *pièce de résistance* at the moment for couples is the fairy light backdrop. This is normally positioned behind the top table or perhaps the band. They generally run in size from about six feet to twenty-four feet and range from about €500–€2,000. My best advice in this area (as in all) is to stick with reputable companies. Not only will they have the range of products in a variety of colours with matching pieces, they will also have a range of items in various sizes – this is particularly important when it comes to chair covers. Hotel banqueting chairs are not all one size and some chair cover companies will not have the stock or range of sizes to cover size option. Do not find this out on the morning of the wedding. Have measurements sent to your hire company or, better still, have them call out to ensure that the covers fit the chairs well in advance of the big day and before you pay any deposits!

Decoration
A lot of companies have cottoned on to the fact that couples now have increasingly larger wedding decoration budgets and so are now catering to this expanding market. Rental and hire companies are now starting to branch into areas other than

furniture, cutlery and linens to include centrepieces, arches, candelabras and much more. Wedding planners and event management companies are now stocking their own ranges of items. Designer and couture weddings are now what most brides aspire to. And with companies catering to these needs with ready-made decor hire packages starting from as little as €575, it is now very achievable.

Top Tip!

Don't forget to ask your photographer to photogaph the special little details you have put so much effort into. You will probably not get to see them all in their unspoiled perfection before the masses descend!

As I am sure you can imagine, the more detail and effort that goes into your decor, the greater amount of coordination required between different companies (florists, lighting specialists, hire companies etc.). For this reason, if your decor is important to you or if it is on a grand scale, I strongly advise you consider hiring a design consultant or wedding designer to help you out, or at the very least, hiring a wedding planner to provide coordination on the wedding day. This will give you peace of mind on the morning of the wedding and will mean that you are not having to take phone calls from suppliers wondering where everything goes!

Words of advice from a planner

When brides come to me for design work, they often think they don't know where to start. I think this is perhaps more fear or a worry that they'll be seen as going 'over the top' with their decor. And then on the other hand, couples have approached me and blatantly said they want to outdo all their friends and for me to work my ultimate magic! Starting with a visit, with just decor in mind, to your ceremony and reception venues is the best way to begin. Look at the locations critically, take photos and notes. Does either location need, or would they benefit from additional decor? This is an important question I always ask my brides and grooms. Less is definitely more in some locations – but that's not to say that you can't still add some wow. Bridal and interior design magazines are a great inspiration for helping you visualise what you want. Following a meeting with us, we prepare mood and picture boards for our couples of the types of direction and style their wedding can head in. If designing your wedding yourself, cut or tear out pictures you like. Keep them all together and then assemble them so that you can show family and friends (or just your fiancé) what you would like. It's a fun way of keeping all your ideas together and a great memento for your 'keepsake' box when the wedding is over.

Once you have all your decisions made and you know what it is you want, it is now time to source all the elements, and at the prices you want to pay! An alternative to hiring is to buy the majority of the decorative items you want. This will obviously be the more expensive option, but if there are a number of friends or family getting married in quick succession they may use the same and share the costs with you. Or you can just sell on yourself once the wedding is over. If you do decide on one or other of these options, remember you will need to have someone, either venue staff or a friend, who can decorate the venue(s) with your purchases.

Remember ...
Regardless of whether you are going for the big wow factor or just keeping it simple, the wedding decor should flow. While every aspect doesn't have to be exactly the same, or even similar in make or colour, their design principle and style should carry effortlessly throughout. From your invites to favours, garter to 'out of towner' guest baskets, all aspects should continue with your chosen theme and style. Attention to detail is key to pulling the look off properly!

— 15 —

Snapshots

Capturing the day

LIFE IS MADE UP OF PRECIOUS MEMORIES and your wedding day will be among some of your most treasured. When I was young I used often sneak up to my Mum's room and carefully lift her blue velvet wedding album (no accounting for taste) out of the tissue paper and leaf through the glossy pages for hours. A sniff of a wedding and I would be asking about photos. Photographs are cherished memories and I think no wedding should be without them. Wedding videos or DVDs were not available when my parents married but you can be assured that I would have worn those out too!

I have always hated photos of myself – I think there are few who don't detest their own photos. Despite this, I still insisted on having both a photographer and videographer at my wedding. You put so much work and effort into one day that it's a shame not to have the recorded memories. In my opinion, a good photographer and videographer should be top of your list.

The right one at the right price
Hiring professional photographers and videographers can be a costly business. Prices can range from €700–€5,000 each, and

beyond. There are, as with most wedding-related areas, plenty of options. Shopping around is key! I find that Dublin-based photographers tend to be on the pricier side – this will no doubt have something to do with higher rents and expenses that they bear opposed to their country couterparts.

Finding the right style of photography and a photographer who is easy to work with is important. While awards and accreditations indicate quality and professionalism, they can also indicate higher prices.

When hiring my own photographer I had my heart set on one in particular. I had seen many of her pictures in various bridal publications and she seemed to capture exactly what I had in mind for my book of memories. Alas, it was not to be. She was booked for my wedding date, and as no other date would do for hubby-to-be I moved on. I contacted several Dublin-based photographers and considered countless until I saw their pricing. My ever-increasing budget was spiralling out of control, and so, in an effort to tame the wild beast, I started to look elsewhere. At a friend's wedding I just fell in love with her photographer – he was the nicest man you could meet. The picture set-ups were effortless and everyone was naturally happy – not a staple gun in sight! I hired him on the spot! I knew for definite I had made the right choice when, after the ceremony, when we were still at the altar, he produced a bottle of water and straws and offered my new husband and me a drink. If I hadn't just been wed I would have frogmarched him up the aisle and married him on the spot for that gesture alone!

Despite going for one of his more expensive packages, paying travel expenses from Mayo to Meath and spending over €300 on prints, I still saved a good €500 on some of the basic packages I had been quoted in Dublin.

Wedding albums

In addition to the style and mood of photography you would like, you must also consider what it is you want as a wedding album. Traditionally an album contains somewhere in the region of forty to sixty photos, depending on the package, chosen from a catalogue of up to 500 taken on the day. No easy choice, let me tell you! Increasingly popular nowadays is the CD album, where a couple purchases all the photos on a CD and makes the album themselves. This is a more cost-effective way but does have the downside of not having any unique or specialist photos that can only be created by a professional. But it is great for printing multiple copies and sizes if you have the facility for this.

Possibly one of the most affordable, if a little unreliable, ways of having a wedding album is asking a friend and/or family member who is good at pointing a lens to take them. There are, of course, drawbacks to this option: you are reliant on them remembering to bring all the required equipment, knowing what is good and bad light, getting the best out of your pictures and knowing how to set up the formal shots and include everyone where appropriate. A professional will know all this naturally, and will be aware of the 'formal' shots that are taken at a wedding.

Remember ...
Compiling a detailed list of your must-have photos and giving this to your photographer will ensure that in addition to countless others you will get the ones you really want. I would recommend this whether you are using a professional or a friend.

A growing trend at weddings now is for disposable cameras to be left on the tables in the dining room for guests to take pictures of each other during the meal and dancing. This can be budget dependable. Disposable cameras range in price from about €4–€6 with developing costs on top of this. Be aware that guests tend to forget to use them, or end up taking pictures of feet or hands in an attempt at humour.

Order of proceedings
Depending on the package you have chosen, a photographer and videographer will normally begin the day's recording at the

bride's house to capture her 'getting ready'. They normally arrive an hour to an hour and a half before the ceremony (depending on distance to the ceremony) and will leave in time to greet the groom arriving at the church, generally thirty minutes before the ceremony. While at the bride's house, they should be discreet and will at times require the bride and various members of the wedding party to pose for various formal pictures, so you should endeavour to be ready a little early to be available for these shots.

Again depending on the package you have chosen, the photographer will normally leave just before the wedding breakfast begins. Unless they are staying on later or it has otherwise been arranged, there is no need to provide a meal for the photographer. If the videographer (and/or any other key personnel who have been with you all day, such as a wedding planner) is staying past the meal to the first dance or beyond, it is advisable to provide them with sustenance. I discourage seating them with guests as those they are seated with are generally offended to be sat with 'the hired help'. It is perfectly acceptable to arrange with the hotel for them to have some food in the bar or a separate room. A modest dinner and non-alcoholic drink and tea or coffee is more than sufficient and should only add in the region of €15–€20 per person.

Your videographer should blend in with the furniture. You should not really notice their presence, unless you have opted for a documentary-style video wherein they will ask you leading questions or you and your guests will talk directly to the camera for the evening. However, this may not be easy on such a day, and it may only suit to have a quick comment from the both of you. The videographer will move amongst guests and proceedings, capturing the day as best they can. If you have organised special entertainment or unusual events, be sure to let your photo-grapher and/or videographer know about them so they can be prepared to capture them.

Again, Appendix IV, pp. 206–209 details some very useful questions you'll need to ask your prospective photographer/videographer.

— 16 —

Show Stoppers

Organising the entertainment

WHEN MY PARENTS GOT MARRIED my father and his friends provided the music with guitars, whistles and banjos. When I got married we hired choirs, pianists, Irish dancers, German entertainers and a DJ. Nowadays it seems that weddings have evolved into shows separate from the main event – the marriage.

It is traditional for your wedding ceremony to be accompanied by music, for the guests to be entertained by a good band following the meal and for aunts and uncles to give out about the volume of the DJ at the afters. But it seems nowadays that we are going above and beyond this.

My brides and grooms commonly ask for their weddings to be different and unique. And while I try to explain to them that their day will be (and is) unique simply because it is *their* wedding day, they just want more. I often find that for those who perhaps do not have the budget for a wow decorative wedding, the music and entertainment section is an excellent area to give them the 'difference' they so desperately crave. After all, it is pretty much assumed that all weddings will have music and/or entertainment of some description. (None of my couples have gone for my 'no music at all' suggestion as an attempt at difference!)

Dum dum di dum

Nearly every woman is familiar with the Wedding March, and while it may not be your choice to walk down the aisle to, it is definitely recognisable. Your wedding day is one of those days when the music played should send shivers down your spine. Every song should instantly transport you back to your magical day when you hear it on the radio in ten years' time. And this is so true of your wedding ceremony music. I should point out that for those who are having a religious ceremony, your priest and a seasoned wedding musician will be able to advise you on the appropriate choices of music for the ceremony. After all, it is a religious sacrament and certain songs/tunes that you may be considering may not be allowed. The priest will have the final say here. (I've also given some supplemenary information in Appendix 11, pp. 167–169.)

Dancing the night away

The music options for the evening are endless. From quartets to bag pipers to jazz duos, five-piece bands to retro DJs, the mind just boggles. It really all comes down to taste, style of music, space and budget.

Before setting your heart on a particular performer, it is best to first establish any limitations your venue(s) may impose on your choices. Some (not many) venues do not allow audio played past a certain time or at all. And others may simply not have the space or facilities to accommodate your choice. Once you know what the situation is, it is best to get as many quotations, details of work and samples as you can.

As well as the band and the DJ, music can be played during the drinks reception and during the meal, as well as during the interval between the band finishing and the DJ starting. Don't get panicked by this. You can very comfortably get away with just hiring a musician for the church and then a DJ for after the meal until the end of the night and still have a musically fantastic day! It is like with every aspect of a wedding – you can really push the boat out if you so wish!

Whether relating to the ceremony or the afters, most seasoned wedding musicians will have websites detailing past work and experience, style and genre of music, audio clips or options to request a demo CD. Before making contact, you should check these out first to make sure they are of the quality and style you want. With bands and DJs it can be particularly hard for you to determine whether or not they are good and while, no doubt, they will have testimonials to the effect that the 'dance floor was full all night', it is no guarantee that they are suitable for your friends and family. With this in mind, when you are making contact, ask when they are next playing/performing so that you can see them in action. It is not uncommon for future brides and grooms to pop their heads into the afters of other weddings to check out the bands! This is perfectly normal and most likely the band will have cleared it with the couple in advance. (On a side note, if this is something you would prefer not happening at your wedding, do let the band/DJ know.)

When hiring any musician for your wedding, if there is a particular piece of music/song you would like played, be sure they know it, or at least of it, and that they are prepared to learn it in advance. Generally the 'set list' of music is not finalised until a month or two in advance of your wedding and if you bring it up then it may be too late. Ensure that the musician/band/DJ is familiar with the venue, that they do not require any specific cabling, amps, lighting etc. Agree set-up times, approximate start times and payment details in advance so that you are all clear. Check with the hotel that the set-up and start times are suitable and that they are happy with your choices. Some venues, either through bad experience, reputation etc. will not allow certain bands/DJs on their premises. Be sure this is not the case with your choice.

Booking and costing

I know from experience that while we all want the best from our music and musicians, the best often means high demand and/or big bucks. And, unfortunately, demand is definitely an issue with good musicians. Realistically, bands need to be booked twelve to eighteen months in advance; the same with some DJs. Church musicians can sometimes be left to eight to twelve months in advance, but be aware that your choices will be limited.

Cost is a big factor with hiring musicians for your wedding. You have only to type in 'average cost of band' on any of the wedding websites and you'll discover numerous discussions on the topic. Cost of musicians will be largely based on the size of the group and the distance to be travelled. Below you will find a rough guide on what you can expect to pay for the various groupings.

CHURCH
Soloist & Accompanist(s)   €400–€800
Quartet   €600–€950
Small Choir   €800–€1,500
Gospel Choir   €1,000+

DRINKS RECEPTION
Soloist & Accompanist(s)   €400–€800
Pianist/Musician (single)   €250–€550
Jazz Combination (duo, trio etc.)   €350–€900

AFTERS
Band   €1,100–€3,000
                 (Realistic average €1,700–€2,600)
DJ   €250–€700
                 (Realistic average €300–€550)

A lot of musicians now offer package combinations, whereby you can hire them for both the church and drinks reception and as band and DJ; some even offer complete day packages. There are, of course, pros and cons to this. The obvious pro is the savings to be had, and the fact that you only have to deal with one supplier for a large portion of the day. A major con to having the same musician (in varying formats) throughout the day is their ability to be energetic throughout the day and right till the end. The church and drinks reception are clearly sombre affairs and there is no need for great enthusiasm or involvement and interaction with the guests, so to have the same musician for both of these is very practical. However, your band and DJ is a different story. These are the guys that are really going to get your party started! You want them to be vivacious, energetic, on top of their game, and while as a band they will be, if you have chosen to keep a member on (most likely the sound engineer or lead vocalist) as a DJ, he is going to be tired after a two to three-hour set with the band. It is just something to bear in mind.

> **Remember ...**
> Get everything in writing: times of set-up and start, price, anything that you/the hotel will have to provide by way of equipment. It's the best way to ensure you'll get what you've paid for.

Other entertainment

Aside from the above, your other options for wedding 'entertainment' is varied. Having Irish dancers perform a small set and then dance with the guests is very popular. This normally lasts about thirty minutes and costs in the region of €500–€700+ depending on the number of dancers.

In addition to these, other options include ballet dancers, belly dancers, caricaturists, comedians, magicians and really any other form of entertainment you can image. Anything is possible, for a fee. Again, we come back to expense. These forms of entertainment are a relatively new fashion in weddings, and with or without, your wedding will still be a major success. Cost-wise, it really is all dependant on the level of travel involved for the artist and the duration of the act. At an approximate value, you are looking to pay from €250–€700 per performer for an act ranging from thirty minutes to two hours.

An alternative idea to having a band at your reception is to follow the wedding breakfast with a casino-themed evening and finish with a DJ. A popular choice at Christmas and staff parties, packages are available from one to three hours, with all equipment, fake money, staff, lighting and audio provided with or without an MC. No 'real money' bets are accepted, but prizes in the form of bottles of champagne are awarded by the organisers. Prices compare relatively well with band hire and you should expect to pay in the region of €1,800–€4,000 depending on the number of guests and length of play. It's definitely not a style that would suit every wedding, or indeed every guest, but it is definitely an alternative option. Once the betting has finished up, the evening can be finished off with a DJ to fill the dance floor.

DIY entertainment

I am now going to talk about DIY options, as in some instances these can be real show cases and others real show stoppers. We all have a friend or family member who can sing a song or play a tune. They are rolled out at family events and everyone, as standard practice, oohs and ahhs and compliments them on how talented they are. Of course, this can be a cost-effective way of providing the music or entertainment for your wedding, but be sure that yours is not their first public performance. Also, be sure that they have the ability, skills and equipment to perform whatever aspect of the day they have so generously volunteered to do. A musician in my youth, I have often been the 'rolled out' relative and played at many cousins' wedding ceremonies. And while I have (modest) confidence in my own abilities, the overall 'effect' of DIY music can be damaged if even only one's playing is substandard. If the services have been 'offered' as opposed to being sought, requesting them to perform an audition is perfectly acceptable, or giving them a small slot as the secondary church musician or as 'interval' band is a nice compromise, keeping all the aunties happy! Even announce it as their debut performance! At all times, remember family politics!

In addition to your potentially musically talented relatives, look at other possibilities or talents that may be lurking amongst you. Dancers, story tellers, mime artists … all these people can be called upon to perform 'as a gift'! Or even overseas friends or relatives can be asked to perform some traditional or cultural piece. My father's best friend has lived in Germany for as long as I can remember. He is married to a lovely German lady and they in turn have the most wonderful German friends. My parents visit often and have themselves made friends with couples out there, who over the years have invited them to children's weddings. It was only polite for them to do the same when I was married. And they brought with them perhaps the best entertainment of the evening. As I have mentioned before, Ireland is the only place in which the civil and religious ceremony take place together. In Germany they are held over two or three days and the wedding becomes a weekend-long event. In order to add diversity to the two to three-day celebrations, Germans play 'wedding games' during their receptions. Primarily they are centred on the bride and groom with some guest participation. They are also normally done without the knowledge of the bride and groom, which adds to the fun of the game. The German couples who attended my wedding played such a game with us.

During the dancing, Lillian (one of the German guests) asked the DJ if she could borrow the mic to share some 'wifely' secrets with me. She said that she had just been talking to James, my husband, and he had said that I hated ironing (which is true). She was now going to let me in on an age-old housewife secret about ironing. She asked James to join her on the dance floor and to remove his jacket and his waistcoat. She went on to say that it was only necessary to iron the parts of a shirt that people were actually going to see, and as James wore a suit to work it was not necessary to iron the back (sure that's no secret, I thought). She then produced a scissors, and started to cut off the back of his shirt! My heart stopped! I stood there in disbelief, and she continued that, as you don't see the arms, you only need to iron the cuffs. She then cuts the arms off his shirt. At this point I was snow white and having heart palpitations at her cutting up his €300 wedding shirt. I was speechless for the first time in my life. She then said, 'You probably don't believe that everyone does this', and she then asked several of my uncles, cousins and male friends to join us on the dance floor and remove their jackets. All are wearing armless, backless shirts and then they all proceeded to dance the Full Monty! It's definitely not an aspect of my wedding that my guests or I will forget in a hurry! It's all about thinking laterally and using your available options. Now, I'll admit I didn't know about this specific aspect of my wedding as my mother had made all the arrangements with them, but unique ideas are lurking in your midst – you just have to find them!

— 17 —

I Now Call On ...

Making the perfect speech

PUBLIC SPEAKING TERRIFIES ME. My mouth goes dry, my palms grow sweaty and I get all dizzy. And I know I am not alone. During the elation of the announcement of your forthcoming wedding, few fathers of the bride or recently appointed best men instantly think of the speech. After the celebrations have died down and both have been sober for more than twenty-four hours, the niggling feeling starts to creep in.

The thoughts of standing in front of 100+ guests can turn any normally coherent and articulate person into a bumbling fool, and while we all sit back and enjoy the charming anecdotes and childhood memories which have been so carefully selected, they are secretly dying a million deaths inside.

The speeches are both dreaded and anticipated. On average there are four speeches at any given wedding – the father of the bride, the father of the groom, the groom and the best man, and they normally occur in that order. It is generally the case that the best man acts as Master of Ceremonies (MC) throughout the day, introducing the bride and groom, the speeches, reading out any faxes and making any formal announcements. In the case that he is not comfortable with this, the duties most likely then pass to your wedding planner or hotel manager/coordinator. Don't worry – your best man is not expected to know what to do nor when to do it and most hotels and/or your planner will have prompted him in advance.

When to have the speeches?

Wedding speeches can take place before, during or after the meal. Some hotels or venues are set in their format for the evening – this will be due to cooking times or staff shifts. If you want your speeches to take place at a very specific part of the evening it is best to make your venue aware of this well in advance so that any necessary arrangements can be made. There are pros and cons no matter at what stage you have the speeches.

Having the speeches during the meal may drag out the service of the meal and play havoc with trying to get everyone served during the allotted time. It also makes it difficult for those giving the speeches to enjoy their meal.

During the dessert, while the tea and coffee is being served or shortly thereafter, is when the speeches begin following a meal. I personally think this is a bad time – most people could do with a break to stretch their legs, have a cigarette or go to the loo and you may find you are waiting around for the majority of people to return before you can begin.

For these reasons I personally prefer and recommend before the meal. There are several reasons for this.

* *It is possibly the one part of the evening where most guests will remain seated and there will be few interruptions, like trips to the bar or toilet and cigarette breaks.*
* *Having the speeches before the meal means those performing a speech can then sit back and relax, knowing their duty is done and not having to watch their alcohol intake or have their nerves at them.*

☀ *Speakers will be inclined to keep their speeches short and snappy, knowing that they have over 100 hungry guests eyeballing them.*

As the bride and groom, you will most likely not hear the speeches of either fathers or the best man before the wedding. They are generally kept top secret both for the surprise element and so they cannot be upstaged. If you are concerned about their content or how good or bad they are, perhaps speak with a close friend who can be trusted to vet them and steer them clear of any inappropriate content or stories you would like left out.

Brides have been known to write all the speeches for each speaker! And I will confess to writing my own husband's! This was more of a collaboration than me handing him what I wanted said, though!

Length of speeches

In total, the speeches should be kept to about twenty minutes. This gives each speaker approximately five minutes to make their speech. There are numerous publications on the art of writing and delivering a speech, as well as publications specific to wedding speeches. Typing 'wedding speeches' into any internet search engine will bring up a list of sites offering speeches for any occasion, tips, hints and suggestions on appropriate content and jokes. See Chapter 21 for a list of some of the best websites for the job, and Chapter 20 for some useful books.

— SECTION FOUR —
Delegating

— 18 —

Taking Responsibility

Who does what and when?

IT COMES WITH THE TERRITORY that friends and family will be involved in your preparations and your big day to a certain degree. Besides those who will offer their services or take it upon themselves to help out, there are a number of people with prescribed tasks. Mostly I refer to those in the wedding party.

The best man, groomsmen, chief bridesmaid, bridesmaids, flowergirls, page boys and ushers will all have tasks to do, whether they know about them or not. It is important to remember that many people will not be aware of what is involved or expected of them when they excitedly accept their roles. And nor in some cases will the discerning bride and groom know what they can and should ask their gracious friends to do.

What follows is a brief list of the expected duties of the various individuals.

Bridesmaids

* *Assist in the selection of the bridesmaid dresses*
* *Provide measurements to the bride for the bridesmaid dresses*
* *Host/co-host the bridal shower and/or hen party*
* *Help pack and address the wedding invitations*
* *Attend pre-wedding parties, if applicable*
* *Pay for dress, shoes and accessories*
* *Pay for transportation to and from the wedding town and/or accommodation*
* *Help the bride get dressed and ready on the wedding day*
* *Help the bride in any tasks or errands*
* *Participate in the bouquet toss, if single.*

Chief Bridesmaid

* *Hosts/co-hosts the bridal shower and/or hen party*
* *Provides measurements to the bride for dress*
* *Helps pack and address the wedding invitations*
* *Helps the bride get dressed and ready on the wedding day*
* *Attends pre-wedding parties, if applicable*
* *Pays for dress, shoes and accessories*
* *Pays for transportation to and from the wedding town and/or accommodation*
* *Helps the bride in any tasks or errands*
* *Participates in the bouquet toss, if single*
* *Holds the groom's wedding ring*
* *Arranges the bride's veil and train during the processional, ceremony and recessional*
* *Makes sure the bride looks perfect for all the pictures*
* *Holds the bride's bouquet during the exchanging of wedding rings*
* *Witnesses the signing of the marriage certificate.*

Flowergirls/Page Boys

* *(Parents) Pay for attire*
* *(Parents) Pay for transportation to and from the wedding town and/or accommodation.*
* *Carry a small basket full of flowers down the aisle and scatter petals*
* *Participate in bridal party picture opportunities*
* *Attend the rehearsal (but not necessarily the rehearsal dinner).*

Groomsmen and Ushers

- *Provide measurements to the groom for the tuxedo rental*
- *Pay for tuxedo and/or shoe rental*
- *Attend pre-wedding parties, if applicable*
- *Welcome guests to the church (and then ask if guest is part of bride's or groom's party. Bride's guests are seated on the left; groom's on the right)*
- *Seat the eldest guests first if a large group arrives*
- *Escort female guests with right arm with her escort walking behind, or lead a couple to their seat*
- *Distribute programmes to guests after they have been seated*
- *Balance out the guests by asking arriving guests if they wouldn't mind sitting on the other (less filled) side*
- *Direct guests to the reception and hand out preprinted maps and directions to those who need them*
- *Participate in the garter toss, if single*
- *Pay for transportation to and from the wedding town and/or accommodation.*

Now you will see from the above that I have put in each task list that the necessary attendant should pay for their own attire. If you are asking them to do this, inform them early on of such. It has slowly become the custom for brides and grooms to foot the bill for all wedding attire for the wedding party (except the mothers and fathers, unless the fathers are wearing the same hired suits as the groomsmen).

Remember ... it's your day – not theirs

It is important to remember that no one is going to take your wedding as seriously as you do, nor will they put as much work and effort into it as you will (except, of course, for your wedding planner!) When it comes to weddings, brides can often become unrealistic in their expectations of their bridesmaids. I've heard of brides asking their bridesmaids to sign contracts in which clauses include: losing a specified amount of weight prior to the wedding; not putting on more than 7lbs prior to the wedding; consulting the bride about all further hair colour and cuts prior to the wedding; not falling pregnant prior to the wedding, and so on. Extreme, you may think ... but it does happen!

No doubt your friends and sisters will be thrilled that you thought of them to stand with you on your big day and to share that special involvement with you. However, do not spoil a good friendship for the sake of one day. Best friends and sisters often fall out because a bride thinks they are not giving it their all, and in a fit of fury she demotes them to guest status and a lifelong friendship and closeness is transformed into a cold acquaintance. Before the joyous event that is your engagement took place, everyone in your intimate circle had a full life, and while they are more than happy to help you plan your wedding day, be realistic in your expectations of them and their spare time. If help, time and involvement are high on your list of priorities for your bridesmaids, it might be an idea to discuss with your friends how they can help you and how much time they will have before you assign the roles of bridesmaids.

It is important to give your friends plenty of notice for fittings, shopping trips, meetings and the like, and to not overload them with time-consuming projects. Don't make all your outings with your friends about the wedding either. Resentment can easily derive from seemingly silly situations. Be especially considerate of friends who may be in long-term relationships with no sign of a ring. While they are happy for you, they may be dealing with their disappointment. And remember … there is life outside and after the wedding!

— 19 —

Count Down!

Knowing what to do and when

THERE IS NO CORRECT ORDER in which to plan a wedding, but there are certain aspects that, if not done according to a certain timescale, may cause you problems with availability. Here is a guide to the stages you should work to. Not all these areas will apply to your situation and you may find that you are doing things in reverse. A good idea is to cross out the ones that do not apply to you and tick the boxes as you get through the ones that do.

As soon as possible
[ ] *Tell relatives and close friends your good news!*
[ ] *Decide on the date and place of wedding.*
[ ] *Arrange a meeting with the priest.*
[ ] *Visit various venues; research menus and arrange timing of the day.*
[ ] *Book your venue and caterers.*
[ ] *Set a budget and decide who is doing what. Accept all offers of help!*
[ ] *Consider opening a wedding bank account.*
[ ] *Organise wedding insurance.*

[ ] *Start looking for the dress. Think about what style you want and whether your wedding is traditional or informal, and take into account the time of year. The sooner you start looking the more likely you are to find your perfect style.*

[ ] *Book your photographer. Talk to them about the style you require i.e. posed or candid, black & white or colour. Make sure they know which family group photographs you would like and ask their advice on timings, backgrounds etc.*

[ ] *Book your videographer. Make sure they know of any special moments you would like captured and discuss the timings of the day. Check with the priest if filming inside the church is permitted.*

From 12 months

[ ] *Choose your bridesmaid and best man.*

[ ] *With the help of both sets of parents, draw up a guest list.*

[ ] *Book your honeymoon and your first night's accommodation. If your honeymoon is abroad, check your passports.*

[ ] *Book marquee (if applicable) and wedding transportation.*

From 6 months

[ ] *Order your rings. Consider special inscription.*

[ ] *Arrange a second meeting with the priest. Arrange the order of service and choose readings and hymns.*

[ ] *Book organist, choir etc.*

[ ] *Organise dress fittings.*

[ ] *Choose the bridesmaids' outfits and arrange fitting if necessary.*

[ ] *Order your cake.*

[ ] *Choose a florist and discuss bouquets and colour scheme. Discuss floral arrangements for the church and reception.*

[ ] *Order all the stationery, invitations, order of service, menus, place cards and 'Thank You' cards.*

[ ] *Select and book musicians and/or DJ for your reception. Discuss with them the music you require and ask their advice on what will work. Make sure they know your special favourites (maybe you and your fiancé have a special tune you would like played for your first dance).*

[ ] *Arrange hire of suits for the groom, best man, ushers and fathers.*

From 2 months

[ ] *Post wedding invitations and keep track of acceptance.
Consider sending a directions map and a list of local
accommodation to guests coming from out of town.*

[ ] *Buy accessories e.g. veil, necklace and earrings. Buy shoes and
start breaking them in around the house.*

[ ] *Have a lovely day out shopping with your mum for her outfit,
your going-away outfit and any honeymoon clothes you
want.*

[ ] *Buy your special wedding lingerie and take it (and your shoes)
to your next fitting.*

[ ] *Organise church rehearsal and make sure all parties involved
know when it is.*

[ ] *Book appointments for hair, nails, tanning and make up.*

[ ] *Reconfirm all bookings made earlier.*

[ ] *Buy presents for your attendants and both mothers.*

[ ] *If you are honeymooning abroad, check if any inoculations
are advised.*

From 4 weeks

[ ] *Send out 'Thank You' cards as gifts arrive or keep a careful list
of people to thank after your wedding so no one is forgotten.*

[ ] *Have trial run of make-up and hair with your veil.*

[ ] *Make sure everyone involved in the wedding knows details of
what is happening and when.*

[ ] *Confirm with your caterers the final number of guests, draw up
a seating plan and write the place cards.*

[ ] *Organise currency and travellers cheques for your honeymoon.
Check with your travel agent and arrange to collect tickets.*

[ ] *Check (surreptitiously) that your father, groom and best man
are preparing their speeches.*

[ ] *If ordered, pick up your wedding rings. Make a list of
everything needing collection or delivery in the next two weeks.
Enlist as much help as possible.*

[ ] *Attend rehearsal at the wedding venue. Use this opportunity to
discuss any final details with your attendants. Ask the best
man to take charge of returning any hired clothes – you can't:
you'll be away on your honeymoon!*

From 1 week

[ ] *Confirm all reception arrangements. Confirm cars, band, DJ, flowers and arrange for cake to be delivered to the reception.*

[ ] *Have a facial and other beauty treatments. Get lots of beauty sleep in the week before your big day.*

[ ] *Gather together your wedding ensemble, going-away outfit and pack for your honeymoon.*

The day before

[ ] *Relax — everything is organised; just enjoy the day.*

[ ] *Have a manicure — it will save time tomorrow.*

[ ] *Pack your overnight bag and arrange for baggage to be delivered to the hotel.*

[ ] *You are bound to be excited, but try to have an early night.*

Your wedding day

[ ] *Allow plenty of time to have your hair and make-up done; enjoy being pampered.*

[ ] *Check the flowers arrive or make sure they are collected in plenty of time.*

[ ] *Have a lovely day. Enjoy yourself knowing that all will run smoothly.*

Remember ...

This day is about the commitment you will make with your partner to be with them for the rest of your lives, to love and respect them, and to stick by them through all good times and bad. This is one of the most special days of your life — take time to remember this and to enjoy it.

— SECTION FIVE —
Resources

— 20 —

Further Reading

Useful books

PLANNING EVERY WEDDING is different; it would be impossible to cover every issue or concern. With this in mind, I suggest you take a look at some of the following books.

Books to help you with the wedding ceremony
Oliver Brennan, *To Love and to Cherish*, Veritas, 2006.

Elizabeth Hughes, *On the Way to the Wedding: The Complete Guide to Planning your Wedding Ceremony*, Veritas, 2006.

Pádraig McCarthy, *A Wedding of your Own*, Veritas, 4th ed., 2003.

Brian Magee CM, *Readings for your Wedding*, Veritas, 2nd ed., 1995.

Books to help with everything else!
Georgina Campbell's Ireland for Romantic Weddings & Honeymoons,
Georgina Campbell's Guide Ltd., 2006

Philip Delamore, *The Wedding Dress: A Visual Sourcebook of Over
200 of the Most Beautiful Gowns Ever Made*, Pavilion Books, 2007.

Jane Durbridge, *Bridal Flowers by Jane Durbridge*, Ryland, Peters &
Small Ltd., 2002.

Carolyn Gerin and Stephanie Rosenbaum, *Anti-Bride Etiquette
Guide*, Chronicle Books, 2005.

Natasha Mac Bhaird, *The Irish Bride's Survival Guide*, O'Brien
Press, 2005.

Stephanie Pedersen, KISS *Guide to Planning a Wedding*, DK
Publishing, 2003.

Books on speeches
Jackie Arnold, *Raise Your Glasses, Please*, How To Books Ltd., 2007.

Angela Lansbury, *Wedding Speeches and Toasts: Your Indespensible
Guide to Writing and Giving the Perfect Wedding Speech*, Ward Lock
Ltd., 2002.

Sarah McElwain, *To the Happy Couple: Creating a Great Wedding
Toast with Style*, Chronicle Books, 2006.

Wedding Speeches and Toasts, Cassell Illustrated, 2006.

Searching the Net

Useful websites

I WOULD RECOMMEND YOU take a look at and register with some of the following sites. They are what I call 'all rounders'. They are essentially online guides and aids to planning your wedding yourself. Most will have supplier directories, recommendations, up-coming events and, most importantly, invaluable discussion forums where brides across the country and world can discuss and recommend the highs and lows of planning the wedding day. Most are free to register with, although some do offer a premium package or upgrade facility, usually somewhere in the region of a once-off fee of €25–€50.

www.paweddings.com
www.realweddings.ie
www.simplyweddings.ie
www.theknot.com
www.weddingsireland.com
www.weddingsonline.ie
www.weddingsonawhim.com
www.wishuponawedding.com

After these, ebay.ie and ebay.com are always good for all sorts of everything! What follows are some very useful websites in relation to some of the topics covered in this book.

Chapter 2: Saying 'I Do'
www.accord.ie
www.gettingmarried.ie

Chapter 3: Marriage and the Law
www.citizensinformation.ie
www.groireland.ie

Chapter 4: The Rock
www.diamond.ie
www.diamondsandgoldireland.com

Chapter 6: Money Matters
www.cheap-chic-weddings.com

Chapter 7: Location, Location, Location
www.hiddenireland.com
www.ireland-guide.com
www.marquee.ie
www.marqueehire.ie
www.marqueesireland.com
www.marqueesnationwide.ie
www.marqueeweddingsinireland.com
www.venuesearch.ie
www.weddingsathome.ie

Chapter 8: Destination Weddings
www.weddings-abroad-guide.com/civil-wedding-abroad

Chapter 9: The Wedding Planner
www.distinctiveweddings.ie
www.ezweddingplanner.com
www.weddingsbyfranc.com

Chapter 10: Paper Mates

www.brideandgroomdirect.co.uk
www.daintree.ie
www.messageinabottle.com
www.weddingcrafter.co.uk

Chapter 11: Cutting a Dash

www.bridalsales.ie
www.bridalshoes.com
www.buyandsell.ie
www.dreamsbridalwear.co.uk
www.houseofbrides.com
www.myweddingbox.co.uk

Chapter 12: Making an Entrance

www.chauffeurireland.ie
www.emerald-limo.ie
www.getawayweddingcars.com
www.leinsterlimos.ie

Chapter 13: Feeding Frenzy

www.chefmike.com
www.chocolate.co.uk
www.mywine.ie
www.premierbarhire.ie
www.thewineroom.ie
www.winesdirect.ie

Chapter 14: Setting the Tone

www.allaboutweddings.com
www.enchantedoccasions.ie
www.gotchacovered.ie
www.hireall.ie
www.kmglinen.ie
www.myperfectday.ie
www.receptions.ie
www.reasonableribbon.com

Chapter 15: Snapshots

www.irishphotographers.com
www.weva.com
www.xenaproductions.com

Chapter 16: Show Stoppers

www.audionetworks.ie
www.irishbandslist.com
www.irishweddingentertainment.ie

Chapter 17: I Now Call On ...

www.diyweddingspeech.com
www.speechtips.com
www.weddingspeechbuilder.com

Appendix I

Readings, Gospels and Prayers of the Faithful

Readings and gospel samples taken from Brian Magee CM, Readings for your Wedding *(Veritas, 1995) and Oliver Brennan,* To Love and to Cherish: A Wedding with a Difference *(Veritas, 2006). All readings from the* New Revised Standard Version Bible. *Prayers of the Faithful taken from* http://www.carr.org/~meripper/faith/marriage.htm *and* http://catholic.pcentral-online.net/prayers/catholic-wedding.html.

SOME CHOICES FOR FIRST READING
(TAKEN FROM THE OLD TESTAMENT):

Genesis 1:26-28.31: *Male and Female he created them.*

Genesis 2:18-24: *They become one flesh.*

Genesis 24:48-51.58-67: *Isaac took Rebekah and he loved her. So he was comforted after his mother's death.*

Ruth 1:16-18: *Where you go, I will go.*

Tobit 7:6-14: *May the Lord of heaven, my child, guide and prosper you and grant you mercy and peace.*

Tobit 8:4-8: *Grant that we may grow old together.*

Song of Songs 2:8-10.14.16; 8:6-7: *Love is strong as death.*

Song of Songs 8:6-7: *Set me as a seal upon your heart.*

Sirach 26:1-4.13-16: *Like the sun rising is the beauty of a good wife in her well-ordered home.*

Jeremiah 31:31-34: *I will make a new covenant with the house of Israel and the house of Judah.*

Revelation 19:1.5-9: *Blessed are those who are invited to the marriage supper of the Lamb.*

Proverbs 31:10-13.19-20.30-31: *A woman who fears the Lord is to be praised.*

SOME CHOICES FOR SECOND READING
(TAKEN FROM THE NEW TESTAMENT)

Romans 8:31-35.37-39: *Who will separate us from the love of Christ?*

Romans 12:1-2.9-18: *Present your bodies as a living sacrifice, holy and acceptable to God.*

I Corinthians 6:13-15.17-20: *Your body is a temple of the Holy Spirit.*

I Corinthians 12:31-13:8: *If I do not have love, I gain nothing.*

Ephesians 5:2.21-33: *This is a great mystery, and I am applying it to Christ and the Church.*

Colossians 3:12-17: *Above all, clothe yourselves with love, which binds everything together in perfect harmony.*

1 Peter 3:1-9: *All of you, have unity of spirit, sympathy, love for one another.*

1 John 3:18-24: *Let us love in truth and action.*

1 John 4:7-12: *God is love.*

Romans 15:1b-3a.5-7.13: *May God grant you to live in harmony with one another.*

Ephesians 4:1-6: *Maintain in unity of the Spirit in the bond of peace.*

Philippians 4:4-9: *The peace of God, which surpasses all understanding, will guard your hearts.*

Some Choices for Gospel Reading

Matthew 5:1-12: *Rejoice and be glad, for your reward is great in heaven.*

Matthew 5:13-16: *You are the light of the world.*

Matthew 7:21.24-29: *He built his house on rock.*

Matthew 19:3-6: *What God has joined together, let no one separate.*

Matthew 22:35-40: *This is the greatest and first commandment. And the second is like it.*

Mark 10:6-9: *They are no longer two, but one flesh.*

John 2:1-11: *Jesus did this, the first of his signs, in Cana of Galilee.*

John 15:9-12: *Abide in my love.*

John 15:12-16: *This is my commandment, that you love one another.*

John 17:20-26: *That they may become completely one.*

Sample Prayers of the Faithful

For N. and N., that their love for each other may continue to grow in the peace of Christ.

For the parents of N. and N., that they may be an example of love to their children.

For all married couples here today, that, witnessing N. and N. making their commitment of love, they renew their love for one another.

For N. and N. who now celebrate with us their joy and gratitude in receiving God's gift of love in the Holy Sacrament of Matrimony, that they may grow old together by sharing life's joys, struggles and challenges in order to become better persons and Christians, especially to those they will touch and experience in their new lives. May the blessings of the Lord guide them through their lives as husband and wife.

For the parents of N. and N., who have given much of themselves to raise their children in the way God had intended, that he may bless them with good health and peace of mind.

For the family, relatives and friends, who have been there to love and support N. and N. through the years. Bless them with God's love and peace always. We pray that God may grant them the happiness that they seek.

For all that are gathered here today to celebrate with N. and N., especially those who have travelled a great distance; that God will bless them and watch over them.

For the deceased relatives and friends of N. and N., that God may shower them with eternal love.

For our loved ones who have gone ahead of us, that they may find eternal rest and happiness in the heavenly kingdom.

For the Holy Church and her leaders, Pope Benedict XVI, our Bishop N., and all our bishops, clergy and religious, that by their words and witness, they may continue to build God's kingdom of justice, peace and unity.

Appendix II

Music for your Ceremony

Adapted from Padraig McCarthy's A Wedding of Your Own *(Veritas, 2003).*

Some points to consider when choosing the music for your wedding ceremony:

There are many different styles of church music: childhood hymns, traditional and folk hymns, classical. When choosing music for the marriage ceremony, you must ask yourself, 'Does it express our faith in God and in Jesus'?

In choosing the music for your church wedding, you will want to consult together, along with the officiating priest or other minister, and the person or persons who will lead in the music area of the celebration. It is good to have musicians who are familiar with music of the liturgy – they may have extra suggestions, and will be more likely to know what is appropriate. It does not have to be all 'wedding music' – other music for liturgical celebrations is also good, and may be well known.

Sample classical music for the wedding ceremony

'Bridal Chorus from *Lohengrin*' (Richard Wagner) (also known as 'Here Comes the Bride')

'Canon in D' (Johann Pachelbel)

'Largo' (from *Guitar Concerto in D Major*) (Antonio Vivaldi)

'Air' (from *Water Music Suite*) (George Frederic Handel)

'The Prince of Denmark's March' (Trumpet Voluntary in D major) (Jeremiah Clarke)

'Procession of Joy' (Hal Hopson)

'Rigaudon' (Andre Campra)

'Wedding March' (from *The Marriage of Figaro*) (Wolfgang Amadeus Mozart)

'Prelude' (from *Te Deum*) (Marc-Antoine Charpentier)

'Trumpet Tune and Air' (Henry Purcell)

'Coronation March for Czar Alexander III' (Peter I. Tchaikovsky)

'Overture' (from *Royal Fireworks Music*) (George Frederic Handel)

'Promenade' (from *Pictures at an Exhibition*) (Modest Mussorgsky)

'Sinfonia' (from *Cantata No. 29*) (Johann Sebastian Bach)

'Sinfonia' (from *Cantata No. 156*) (Johann Sebastian Bach)

'Prelude and Fugue in C' (Johann Sebastian Bach)

'Toccata' (from *L'Orfeo*) (Claudio Monteverdi)

'Romance from String Quartet' (Wolfgang Amadeus Mozart)

'Piano Concerto No. 21 in C major' (Wolfgang Amadeus Mozart)

'Trumpet Tune in A-Major' (David N. Johnson)

'Wedding March' (from *Incidental music, A Midsummer Night's Dream, Op. 61*) (Felix Mendelssohn)

'Winter', Largo or 'Spring', Allegro (from *The Four Seasons*) (Antonio Vivaldi)

Traditional hymns

Wherever You Go (Rob Allison)

Ag Críost an Síol (Music by Seán Ó Riada)

Ave Maria (Franz Schubert)

Ave Verum Corpus (Mozart)

Lord of All Hopefulness (Jan Struther)

I Will Be The Vine (Liam Lawton)

Make Me a Channel of Your Peace (Words by Sebastian Temple)*

Bind Us Together (Words by Bob Gillman)**

Peace, Perfect Peace (Words by Edward Bickersteth; Music by George Caldbeck and Charles Vincent)

Peace I leave with you (M. Ryan Taylor)

Panis Angelicus (Thomas Acquinas)

Jesu, Joy of Man's Desiring (Myra Hess)

Also check out Liam Lawton's CD *A Day of Our Own: Music for a Wedding Liturgy* (Veritas, 2004) and Margaret Daly (ed.), *Music for Your Wedding*, songbook and CD (Veritas, 2004).

* © Copyright 1967 OCP Publications; copyright permission must be sought to reproduce the text.

** © Copyright 1977 Thankyou Music/Kingswaysong. Adm. by worshiptogether.com songs, excl. Europe and UK, adm. by kingswaysongs.com; copyright permission must be sought to reproduce the text.

Appendix III

Sample Mass Booklet

Welcome to the Marriage Ceremony
of
ANNE MARIE WALKER AND PATRICK DUNNE

At the Church of the Immaculate Conception,
Ashbourne, Co. Meath

Friday 8 August 2008 at 2 p.m.

Thank You to:

Celebrant: N.

Best Man: N.

Groomsman: N.

Bridesmaids: N.

Flowergirls: N.

Page boys: N.

Readers: N.

Prayers of the Faithful: N.

Music: N.

Introduction

PRIEST: In the name of the Father and of the Son and of the Holy Spirit.

ALL: Amen.

PRIEST: The Lord be with you.

ALL: And also with you.

Penitential Rite

PRIEST: My brothers and sisters, to prepare ourselves to celebrate the sacred mysteries let us call to mind our sins.

ALL: I confess to Almighty God and to you my brothers and sisters that I have sinned through my own fault, in my thoughts and in my words, in what I have done and what I have failed to do: and I ask the blessed Mary ever Virgin, all the angels and saints and you, my brothers and sisters, to pray for me to the Lord our God.

PRIEST: May almighty God have mercy on us, forgive us our sins and bring us to everlasting life.

ALL: Amen.

PRIEST: Lord have mercy.

ALL: Lord have mercy.

PRIEST: Christ have mercy.

ALL: Christ have mercy.

PRIEST: Lord have mercy.

ALL: Lord have mercy.

Gloria

ALL: Glory to God in the highest and peace to his people on earth. Lord God, heavenly King, almighty God and Father, we worship you, we give you thanks, we praise you for your glory. Lord Jesus Christ, only Son of the Father, Lord God, Lamb of God, you take away the sins of the world: have mercy on us; you are seated at the right hand of the Father, receive our prayer. For you alone are the Holy One, you alone are the Lord, you alone are the most high, Jesus Christ, with the Holy Spirit, in the glory of God the Father. Amen

Opening Prayer

PRIEST: *Let us pray:* Father, you have made the bond of marriage a holy mystery, a symbol of Christ's love for his Church. Hear our prayers for Anne Marie and Patrick. With faith in you and in each other they pledge their love today. May their lives always bear witness to the reality of that love. We ask this through our Lord Jesus Christ, your Son,

who lives and reigns with you and the Holy Spirit,
one God for ever and ever.

ALL: Amen.

Liturgy of the Word
FIRST READING

A reading from the Book of Ruth (1:16-18)

But Ruth said: Do not press me to leave you or to turn back
from following you! Wherever you go, I will go; where you
live, I will live; your people shall be my people and your God
will be my God too. Wherever you die, I will die - there will
I be buried. We shall live together forever and our love will
be the gift of our life.

This is the word of the Lord.

ALL: Thanks be to God.

RESPONSORIAL PSALM

*Response: My Beloved is mine and I am his. He pastures his
flock among the lilies.*

My Beloved lifts up his voice,
he says to me,
'Come then, my love,
my lovely one, come.
For see, winter is past,
the rains are over and gone'. R

The flowers appear on the earth.
The season of glad songs has come,
the cooing of the turtledove is heard
in our land.
The fig tree is forming its first figs
and the blossoming vines give out their fragrance. R

Come then, my love,
my lovely one, come.
My dove, hiding in the clefts of the rock,
in the coverts of the cliff,
show me your face,
let me hear your voice;
for your voice is sweet
and your face is beautiful. R

SECOND READING

A reading from the letter of St Paul to the Romans (12:9-12)
Do not let your love be a pretence, but sincerely prefer good
to evil. Love each other as much as brothers should, and
have a profound respect for each other. Work for the Lord
with untiring effort and with great earnestness of spirit. If
you have hope, this will make you cheerful. Do not give up
if trials come; and keep on praying. If any of your friends
are in need you must share with them. And you must make
hospitality your special care.
This is the word of the Lord.
ALL: Thanks be to God.

Gospel Acclamation
ALL: Alleluia, Alleluia,
          As long as we love one another
          God will live in us.
          And his love will be complete in us.
          Alleluia.

GOSPEL READING
PRIEST: The Lord be with you.
ALL: And also with you.
PRIEST: A reading from the Holy Gospel according to
          John.
ALL: Glory to you, Lord.

Jesus to his disciples: 'This is my commandment: that you love one another as I have loved you. No one has greater love than to lay down one's life for one's friends. You are my friends if you do what I command you. I do not call you servants any more, because a servant does not know what the master is doing; I call you friends because I have made known to you everything that I have heard from my Father. You did not choose me but I chose you. And I appointed you to go and bear fruit, fruit that will last. And then the Father will give you whatever you ask him in my name. What I command you is to love one another.

This is the Gospel of the Lord.

All: Praise to you, Lord Jesus Christ.

The Rite of Marriage

The priest addresses Anne Marie and Patrick.

PRIEST: Anne Marie and Patrick, you have come to this church so that the Lord may seal your love in the presence of the priest and this community. Christ blesses this love. He has already consecrated you in baptism; now by a special sacrament, he strengthens you to fulfil the duties of your married life.

Anne Marie and Patrick, you are about to celebrate this sacrament. Have you come here of your own free will and choice without compulsion to marry each other?

BOTH: We have.

PRIEST: Will you love and honour each other in marriage all the days of your life?

BOTH: We will.

PRIEST: Are you willing to accept, with love, the children God may give you and bring them up in accordance with the law of Christ and his Church?

BOTH: We are.

Declaration of Consent

PRIEST: I invite you then to declare before God and his Church your consent to become husband and wife.

Patrick : Anne Marie, do you consent to be my wife?

ANNE MARIE:
I do.

ANNE MARIE:
Patrick, do you consent to be my husband?

PATRICK: I do.

They join hands and say together:
We take each other as husband and wife and promise to love each other truly for better, for worse, for richer, for poorer, in sickness and in health, all the days of our life.

PRIEST: What God joins together man must not separate.
May the Lord confirm the consent you have given and enrich you with his blessing.

Blessing of the Rings

PRIEST: Almighty God, bless these rings as symbols of faithfulness and unbroken love.
May Anne Marie and Patrick always be true to each other, may they be one in heart and mind, may they be united in love forever,
Through Christ, our Lord.

ALL: Amen.

PATRICK: Anne Marie, wear this ring as a sign of our faithful love. In the name of the Father, and of the Son and of the Holy Spirit.

ANNE MARIE:
Patrick, wear this ring as a sign of our faithful love. In the name of the Father, and of the Son and of the Holy Spirit.

Exchange of Gifts

BOTH: We accept these coins as a sign of sharing all that
we possess.

Symbol of Unity

Anne Marie and Patrick extinguish the two outer candles and
together light the centre candle, symbolising their unity in
marriage.

PRAYERS OF THE FAITHFUL

N.: For Anne Marie and Patrick, as they begin their
life together and for happiness in their home.
Let us pray to the Lord.

ALL: Lord, hear our prayer.

N.: For the parents, relatives and friends of Anne
Marie and Patrick who have provided them with
support and unconditional love throughout their
lives and who have helped them grow as individuals and as a couple over the years. May they continue to offer love and friendship as they begin
their special journey today.
Let us pray to the Lord.

ALL: Lord, hear our prayer.

N: For absent relatives and friends. We remember
especially N. and N., whom we know are with us
in spirit. May they enjoy perfect happiness and
total fulfilment in eternal life.
Let us pray to the Lord.

ALL: Lord, hear our prayer.

N.: For those who are victims of injustice across the
world through famine, poverty and war, and for
those deprived of love and affection. May the
hearts of humankind be moved to promote justice,
love and peace.

Let us pray to the Lord.

ALL: Lord, hear our prayer.

Liturgy of the Eucharist

OFFERTORY PROCESSION

Mothers of the Bride and Groom take up the gifts.

PRIEST: Pray, brothers and sisters, that our sacrifice may be acceptable to God the almighty Father.

ALL: May the Lord accept the sacrifice at your hands for the praise and glory of his name, for our good and the good of all his Church.

PRAYER OVER THE GIFTS

PRIEST: Lord, accept our offering for this newly married couple, Anne Marie and Patrick. By your life and providence you have brought them together, bless them all the days of their married life. We ask this through Christ our Lord.

ALL: Amen.

EUCHARISTIC PRAYER

PRIEST: The Lord be with you.

ALL: And also with you.

PRIEST: Lift up your hearts.

ALL: We lift them up to the Lord.

PRIEST: Let us give thanks to the Lord.

ALL: It is right to give him thanks and praise.

PRIEST: Father, all-powerful and ever-living God, we do well always and everywhere to give you thanks. You created us in love to share your divine life. We see our high destiny in the love of husband and wife, which bears the imprint of your own divine love. Love is our origin, love is our constant calling, love is our fulfilment in heaven. The love of man and woman is made holy in the Sacrament of Marriage, and becomes the mirror of your everlasting love.

Through Jesus Christ the choirs of angels and all the Saints praise and worship your glory. May our voices blend with theirs as we join in their unending hymn of praise.

All: Holy, Holy, Holy Lord God of power and might, Heaven and earth are full of your glory.

Hosanna in the highest. Blessed is he who comes in the name of the Lord.

Hosanna in the highest.

PRIEST: Let us proclaim the mystery of faith.

ALL: He is Lord, he is Lord.

He is risen from the dead and he is Lord.

Every knee shall bow, every tongue confess, that Jesus Christ is Lord.

Communion Rite

PRIEST: Let us pray with confidence to the Father in the words our Saviour gave us.

ALL: Our Father who art in heaven, hallowed by thy name. Thy kingdom come, thy will be done on earth, as it is in heaven. Give us this day our daily bread, and forgive us our trespasses as we forgive those who trespass against us, and lead us not into temptation, but deliver us from evil.

PRIEST: Deliver us, Lord, from every evil and grant us peace in our day. In your mercy keep us free from sin and protect us from all anxiety as we wait in joyful hope for the coming of our Saviour, Jesus Christ.

ALL: For the kingdom, the power and the glory are yours, now and forever.

Nuptial Blessing

RITE OF PEACE

PRIEST: Lord Jesus Christ you said to your apostles:

I leave you peace, my peace I give you.
Look not on our sins but on the faith of your Church and grant us the peace and unity of your kingdom where you live forever and ever.

ALL: Amen.

PRIEST: The peace of the Lord be with you always.

ALL: And also with you.

PRIEST: Let us offer one another the sign of peace.

PRIEST: May this mingling of the body and blood of our Lord Jesus Christ bring eternal life to us who receive it.

ALL: Lamb of God, you take away the sins of the world, have mercy on us.

Lamb of God, you take away the sins of the world, have mercy on us.

Lamb of God, you take away the sins of the world, grant us peace.

PRIEST: This is the Lamb of God, who takes away the sins of the world; happy are those who are called to his supper.

ALL: Lord, I am not worthy to receive you, but only say the word and I shall be healed.

Prayer After Communion

PRIEST: Let us pray. Lord, in your love you have given us this Eucharist to unite us with one another and with you. As you have made Anne Marie and Patrick one in this sacrament of marriage and in the sharing of one bread and one cup so now make them one in love for each other. We ask this through Christ our Lord.

ALL: Amen.

Concluding Rite

PRIEST: The Lord be with you.

ALL: And also with you.

PRIEST: May God the eternal Father keep you steadfast in your love.

ALL: Amen.

PRIEST: May you have children to bless you, friends to console you and may you live in peace with all people.

ALL: Amen.

PRIEST: May the peace of Christ dwell in your home. May the angels of God protect it and may the holy family of Nazareth be its model and inspiration.

ALL: Amen.

PRIEST: May almighty God bless you, the Father, the Son and the Holy Spirit.

ALL: Amen.

PRIEST: The Mass is ended. Go in peace to love and serve the Lord.

ALL: Thanks be to God.

Appendix IV

Checklists

What follows are some handy checklists to help you keep track of your spending, and forms to guide you in what to ask the various agents and vendors when it comes to booking various elements of your wedding day.

Choosing the Date

Below is designed to help you choose a date quickly and easily by mapping out any other weddings, family events or important days that are coming up so that your big day doesn't clash with anything!

The Year:

2009   2010   2011   2012   2013   2014
2015   2016   2017   2018   2019

Remember to give yourselves plenty of time to plan, save and prepare for the big day.

The Month:

Jan   Feb   Mar   Apr   May   Jun   Jul
Aug   Sep   Oct   Nov   Dec

Remember to avoid clashing with other weddings, family or sporting events. Choose a month that has special memories or choose a brand new one in which to create them!

The Day:

Mon   Tue   Wed   Thu   Fri   Sat   Sun

The day of the week you wed may be chosen for you by a specific date you have already chosen or you may choose a day and by this way come to the corresponding date!

The Date:

1   2   3   4   5   6   7   8   9   10   11   12   13   14   15   16
17   18   19   20   21   22   23   24   25   26   27   28   29   30   31

Finally, your Wedding Date:

Budget Tracker

You can use this budet tracker to list all your predicted and actual expenses in order to keep an eye on things.

Bride	Estimated Cost	Actual Cost
Ring		
Dress		
Veil/Tiara		
Shoes		
Underwear		
Hair Styling		
Make-up		
Nails		
Facial		
Tanning		
Waxing		
Jewellery		
Going Away Outfit		
Other		
Sub Total		

Bridesmaids	Estimated Cost	Actual Cost
Dress		
Shoes		
Hair		
Make-up		
Nails		
Facial		
Tanning		
Other		
Sub Total		

Groom	ESTIMATED COST	ACTUAL COST
Ring		
Suit		
Shoes		
Shirt		
Tie		
Hair/Shave		
Going Away Outfit		
Other		
Sub Total		

Best Man/ Groomsmen	ESTIMATED COST	ACTUAL COST
Suit Hire		
Shoes		
Other		
Sub Total		

Flowergirls & Page Boys	ESTIMATED COST	ACTUAL COST
Dress		
Suit		
Shoes		
Accessories		
Other		
Sub Total		

Flowers	ESTIMATED COST	ACTUAL COST
Bouquets		
Boutonnières		
Ceremony Flowers		
Reception Flowers		
Sub Total		

Transport	ESTIMATED COST	ACTUAL COST
Wedding Cars		
Wedding Bus		
Horse & Carriage		
Other		
Sub Total		

Stationery	ESTIMATED COST	ACTUAL COST
Ceremony Invites		
Evening Invites		
Inserts (RSVP etc).		
Postage		
Ceremony Booklets		
'Thank You' Cards		
Place Cards/ Menus		
Other		
Sub Total		

Photography	ESTIMATED COST	ACTUAL COST
Photographer		
Videographer		
Extra Prints/ Albums		
Disposable Cameras		
Developing Charges		
Sub Total		

Cake ESTIMATED COST ACTUAL COST

Cake
Cake Knife
Other

Sub Total

Ceremony ESTIMATED COST ACTUAL COST

Celebrant's
  Fee
Altar Servers
Sacristan
Singer(s)
Organist/
  Musicians
Other

Sub Total

Reception	ESTIMATED COST	ACTUAL COST
Venue Hire		
Food		
Wine		
Drinks		
Reception		
Champagne		
Toast		
Corkage		
Bridal Suite		
Table		
Decorations		
Favours		
Sub Total		

Reception Entertainment	ESTIMATED COST	ACTUAL COST
Band		
DJ		
Other		
Sub Total		

Misc.	ESTIMATED COST	ACTUAL COST
Confetti/Petals/ Bubbles		
Press Announcements		
Rehearsal Dinner		
Gifts		
Other		
Sub Total		

Totals

Bride
Groom
Bridesmaids
Best Man/Groomsmen
Flowergirls & Page Boys
Flowers
Transport
Stationery
Photography
Cake
Ceremony
Reception
Entertainment
Misc.

Grand Total

Form for Venue Hire

Basic Information

Name:
Address:

Phone Number:
Fax Number:
Email:
Website:
Event Coordinator's Name:
Mobile Number:
Email:
Category (Hotel, Castle, etc.):

Room Configuration

Room Size:

Number of Doors:

Air Conditioning:

Type (Wall, Covering, Colours):

Type (Floor, Covering, Colours):

Type of Sound System:

Type of Lighting:

Location of Air Vents:

Location of Temp Controls:

Phone/T1/CAT 5 Line:

Electrical Outlets:

Electrical Capacity:

Ceiling:

Columns:

Location/Number of Restrooms:

Payphone Location:

Coat Room/Checker:

Location of Kitchen/Back of House:

Rules About Signage:

Rules About Candles:

Rules About other Decor:

Ask for Room Layout Diagrams

Max Room Capacity:

Pre-Convention Area:

Access to Room (Time):

Who Sets What?

Number Rounds/Size Available:

Number Banquet/Size Available:

Number of Serpentines/Available:

Number Chairs/Type:

Chair Cover Style/Colour/Cost:

Available Linens/Size/Colour/Cost:

Available Napkins/Size/Colour:

Table Skirting Colours:

Lecterns/Podiums/Microphones:

Sound System Requirements:

AV Services In-House?

Staging/Risers:

Dance Floor Size/Configuration:

In-House Decor Items:

In-House Centrepieces:

Mirrors:

Candles:

Coat Racks:

Lift Locations:

Storage for Boxes and Presents:

Additional Notes:

FURTHER INFORMATION

Ask for Menus and Special Menus (kosher, veggie, etc.)

Ratio of Wait Staff to Guests:

Number of Bars:

Ratio of Bartenders to Guests:

Bar Minimums:

Drink Pricing:

Corkage Policy:

Left-Over Policy:

Service Charges:

Extra Costs:

Dress Code for Wait/Bar Staff:

Type/Style Dinnerware/Charges:

Bar Extension/Cost:

Music Finish Time:

Parking/Location/Cost:

Valet Service Cost:

Any Construction Plans:

Smoking Policy:

Security:

Noise Policy:

Business Centre/Hours:

Other Events Scheduled:

Additional Information:

HOTEL ROOMS

Number of King-Sized Rooms: €

Number of Double Rooms: €

Number/Type of Suites: €

Presidential Suite: €

Bridal Suite: €

Maid Service (Cost Per Day):   €

Bell Service (Cost Per Day):   €

List of Room Amenities:

Number of Phone Lines:

Data Ports:

Wireless Internet:

Room Description/Condition:

Additional Notes:

On Arrival

Check In/Out Times:

Lobby Area Description:

Bell Stand Services:

Front Desk Services:

Valet/Parking Experience:

Distance from Airport:

Available Public Transport:

Additional Notes:

Food and Beverages

Outlets In-House:

Get Restaurant Menus

Hours of Operation:

Restaurants Close By:

Bars In-House:

Bar/Lounges Close By:

Form for Caterer Hire

BASIC INFORMATION

Company Name:
Address:

Phone Number:
Fax Number:
Email:
Website:
Contact's Name:
Mobile Number:

NECESSITIES

Are you a full-time caterer?

What kind of experience, background and education do
you have?

Have you received any formal training as a caterer/chef?

How long have you been a caterer and how many events
have you catered?

Have you handled events of this type and size before?

Do you have all necessary permits and certifications?

Do you operate a HACCP system?

When was your last Environmental Health Inspection and
what was your result?

Are you properly insured? Please provide a copy of your
insurance policy.

Do you provide tasting consultations/food tastings?

Is there a fee for such tastings?

How many people can attend such tastings?

What time do you normally arrive to set up your equipment?

Hours of service:

What equipment do you provide?

Do you require us to supply any equipment?

What is the staff to guest ratio?

What is the staff dress code, formal or casual?

If buffet style is offered, are servers provided or will it be self-service?

Is there an extra charge for buffet servers; if yes, how much?

Do you have a liquor licence?

Is there any extra charge for barender; if so, how much?

Who is supplying the liquor, water, ice, etc.?

Do you provide cake cutting/serving service?

Do you provide the wedding cake or should I hire an outside baker?

When is the final headcount normally due?

Does this headcount involve wedding professionals at the event (photographer etc.)?

Are there special prices for children?

Are there special prices for feeding our wedding professinals?

Is a deposit required; if so, how much?

May I make partial payments?

Do you provide linen, tables, chairs, china, glassware, silverware, serving accessories etc.?

Are the above items included in the price; if not, how much extra do they cost?

Do you provide a written contract and guarantee?

Are there any additional charges not yet covered (travel etc.)?

What are the refunds/cancellation terms?

What is your leftover policy?

What is your corkage policy?

Do you provide rentals, or are they from another company?

Form for Stationery Agent

BASIC INFORMATION

Company Name:
Address:

Phone Number:
Fax Number:
Email:
Website:
Contact's Name:
Mobile Number:

NECESSITIES

How many designers work for the company?

If the designer sought no longer works for the
company come my wedding, what will you do?

Are you a full-time designer?

What kind of experience, background and education do
you have?

Have you received any formal training as a designer?

From where do you get your inspiration?

Do you have a portfolio and list of references?

Can we see samples of your recent work?

How many weddings have you serviced?

How many weddings do you do a year/a month?

Have you handled events of this size before?

What type of design do you specialise in?

What type of design do you normally suggest for weddings?

Where do you perform the design?

PRODUCTS

Do you design Mass booklets?

Do you design invitations?

Can you handle the postage of invitations, or is there an extra charge?

Do you design 'Thank You' cards?

Do you design place names?

Can you design reply cards?

What is the standard lead time?

What is your normal method of delivery?

Please outline the cost of each of your products for design and print:

BILLING AND LEGAL

Is a deposit required. If so, how much?

When is the deposit due?
Can partial payments be made?

What are the refunds/cancellation terms?

What is the average cost of wedding stationery?

Do you charge for consultations/visitations?

Additional notes:

Form for Transport Arrangements

Basic Information

Company Name:
Address:

Phone Number:
Fax Number:
Email:
Website:
Contact's Name:
Mobile Number:
Type (Horse Drawn Carriage, Limo, Rolls Royce, etc.):

Necessities

Are you fully and properly insured?

Are you affiliated with any national transport associations?

Are you open twenty-four hours a day?

How many and what type of limos do you have?

What is your policy if the limo breaks down?

Can we have alcohol in the vehicles?

Can we eat in the vehicles?

What attire will the chauffeur be wearing?

Does the car have a CD player?

What is the average age of your vehicles?

If required, do they have their NCT?

Are you a member of the AA?

Do the vehicles have air-conditioning/heating?

Do you offer discounts if additional vehicles are booked?

Can I get a signed contract stating the date, time, all locations, prices, type of vehicle including year, make and model, colour, payment, deposit and cancellation policy?

How far in advance do I need to book the service?

Can I pay by credit card, Laser or cheque?

Is a deposit required; if so, how much?

What is the cancellation policy?

Form for Photographer

Basic Information

Name:
Address:

Contact:
Phone Number:
Fax Number:
Mobile Number:
Email:
Website:

Details

What price ranges are your packages?

How many weddings a month would you normally photograph?

How long are you in business?

Will you personally be the photographer for our wedding?

If not, when can we meet the photographer whose work this is so we can see if we feel comfortable with that person/see if we are on the same wavelength?

If the photographer we want no longer works for your studio when our wedding comes up, what will you do?

At what time do you arrive to set up your equipment?

Hours of service:

How many people will cover the event?

Do you bring back-up equipment with you?

What are your policies regarding proofs?

What are your policies regarding negatives?

What are your policies regarding delivery times?

Is a deposit required? If so, how much?

When is the final payment due?

What is the overtime charge?

Are there any additional charges not mentioned (i.e. travel)?

What are the refunds/cancellation terms?

Form for Videographer

Basic Information

Name:
Address:

Contact:
Phone Number:
Fax Number:
Mobile Number:
Email:
Website:

Details

How many weddings a month would you normally video?

How long are you in business?

Will you personally be the videographer for our wedding?

If not, when can we meet the videographer whose work this is so we can see if we feel comfortable with that person/see if we are on the same wavelength?

If the videographer we want no longer works for your studio when our wedding comes up, what will you do?

How many people will cover the event?

How many video cameras will cover the event?

What equipment do you use to edit the video?

What criteria do you use for choosing what you would videotape at my wedding?

Do you conduct interviews with the guests and wedding party?

Set Up

What time do you arrive to set up your equipment?

Hours of service:

Do you bring back-up equipment with you?

Billing and Legal

What price ranges are your packages?

What are your policies regarding proofs?

What are your policies regarding delivery times?

Is a deposit required? If so, how much?

When is the final payment due?

What is the overtime charge?

Are there any additional charges not mentioned (i.e. travel)?

What are the refunds/cancellation terms?

Miscellaneous

Price list

DVD Sample of Work

Appendix V

My Wedding A to Z

A IS FOR Aoife our Maid of Honour.

B IS Bláithín our Blushing Bride.

C IS FOR Confetti. As this is not allowed at our venue we will be providing bubbles as an alternative.

D IS FOR Directions. We've included directions both to the church and to the hotel. These are mainly for our male guests as we know you won't stop to ask!

E IS FOR Etiquette. As we are spending our wedding night at the hotel, please feel free to leave when you are ready and disregard etiquette which traditionally asks you to wait for the Bride & Groom to depart.

F IS FOR Family and Friends. This is what weddings are all about.

G IS FOR Gifts. We mean it when we say that your presence is more important to us than your presents.

H IS FOR Honeymoon. We will be going to Mauritius soon after the wedding.

I IS FOR Important People. We ask that you remember those who are important to us but are unable to join us on the day. They will definitely be in our thoughts.

J IS FOR James, our Gorgeous Groom.

K IS FOR Kids. Weddings are a family occasion. We would love you to bring your children, but we understand if you want to also make this a special occasion for yourselves as a couple.

L IS FOR Love. This is a celebration of our love and we'd like you to be there with us.

M IS FOR Map. As we don't want you to get lost please see enclosed.

N IS FOR nibbles that will be served during the dancing to keep your strength up!

O IS FOR Order of the Day. After our 2 p.m. ceremony there will be drinks and photographs, followed by our wedding breakfast at around 6 p.m. with speeches and cake cutting.

P IS FOR Photographs. Our photographer's name is Alan and he will be with us throughout the day. He is a very nice man so make sure he sees and snaps you!

Q IS FOR Quiet Please! Please turn off any mobile phones during the ceremony and the wedding breakfast.

R IS FOR Roganstown Golf & Country Club, where the reception will be held; details are enclosed.

S IS FOR Smoking. There is a no smoking policy during and after the ceremony within Roganstown. Smoking is permitted in the designated areas outside the venue,

T IS FOR Table Plan. A Table Plan will be displayed in the entrance to the dining hall – please make sure you know which table you should be seated at for the wedding breakfast. Otherwise you may end up with someone else's dinner!

U IS FOR Ushers: they will greet you at the church and show you to your seats.

⤨

X IS FOR eXperience. As this is our first experience organising a wedding please excuse us if we have missed out any important information. Please feel free to call us and ask any unanswered questions.

⤨

Y IS FOR You. As our guest you will help make our wedding a very special day.

⤨

Z IS FOR Zzzzzzzzzs. For those of you that don't live locally I've enclosed a list of hotels and Bed & Breakfasts that you might like to stay in.

Index